Dear Harland and Shirley!

M000094299

THE 24-HOUR
CHAMPION

DISCOVERING AND LIVING YOUR PRICELESS LIFE

May this book bless you two as you both have done for so many. May it also touch you, inspire you and give something back to you both.

Thanks!

DARSHAN G. SHANTI

5/4/10

Darshan G. Shanti

Printed in the United States of America
ISBN: 1-4392-3307-1
ISBN-13: 9781439233078

Visit www.booksurge.com to order additional copies.

Warning – Disclaimer
The purpose of this book is to educate and entertain. The author or publisher does not guarantee
that anyone following the techniques, suggestions, tips, ideas or strategies will become successful. The author and publisher shall have neither liability nor responsibility to anyone with respect
to any loss or damage caused, or alleged to be caused, directly or indirectly by the information
contained in this book.

SOME CELEBRITY POSITIVE PRAISE
AND RAVE REVIEWS

"I was really inspired by The 24-Hour Champion. If you want to turn your life into a masterpiece – this is the guidebook."

– Dr. Joe Vitale, author of The Attractor Factor (2nd addition) and star of the movie, The Secret.

"I have known Darshan for a number of years and I am so overjoyed to see that his vision of The 24-Hour Champion has been born. This book will help you become a committed champion in your own life. We have to have REAL commitment to our dream and this book holds many direct instructions, examples and age-old truths broken down in such a way that YOU can begin immediately to become the greatest you, you can be. It is all within you. Read this book and take action!"

Michele A. Blood co author with Bob Proctor - "Become A Magnet To Money Through The Sea Of Unlimited Consciousness" and "How To Become A Magnet To Hollywood Success" www.musivation.com

"If I could sum up this book in one word, that word would be FREEDOM. More specifically, freedom from your past barriers, beliefs and blocks and freedom to be who you are and live the life you've always wanted, starting right now!'

James Malinchak – Co-Author, Chicken Soup For The College Soul, "Two Time College Speaker of the Year." www.malinchak.com

In the 25 years that I have studied human consciousness and behavior, I have worked with some of the most effective personal development teachers. None of them have put all of these principles into a single book or experience. Had this book been available to me when I started on my path, my life would be even more glorious than it is today.

Jim Campbell, President, Wellness Improvement Experts -www.wellnessimprovementexperts.com

"Thank you for all the emails and words of encouragement and wonder. I have read more books, done more courses, and none has made me feel the way your book has. My longing and wanting this is a deep need to be all that I can be and I want you to know that you have hit the right core with my heart, mind and soul. Your book is wonderful. I relate to each page and can not begin to tell you how much I see myself in what you write. It is the last thing I read at night before switching off the light and the first thing I read in the morning as I open my eyes."

Patricia Jennett Richards, Johannesburg, South Africa

"Some books motivate and inspire. Others give great information. The 24-Hour Champion does both! If you are looking for answers to the questions of why you aren't making the amount of money you think you should, why your relationships are just OK instead of great and why some people live a dream life and yours seems like a nightmare, then get your copy of The 24-Hour Champion.

It's easy to read, yet full of practical wisdom. Not only will you gain a better understanding of why your life isn't exactly how you want it to be, but you will discover EXACTLY what to do to get on track to having the life of your dreams."

Jonathan Zide, Speaker, Author and Marketing Consultant
- ww.marketingdemystified.com

DEDICATION

This book is the culmination of twenty-years of study in the field of human behavior, potential, motivation, inspiration and transformation. During that time I have been influenced, loved, cared for and supported by countless numbers of people. Some came into my life for a while and left on a whisper, some left with a bang and some are still along for the ride. To all of you, I thank you. I love you. I value you and I want you to know that a little bit of each of you is in this book. You all are my champions.

Yet there is one who stands out above and beyond. There is one who has never given up on me... no matter how foolish I was, no matter how stubborn I was, no matter how angry or arrogant I was. She is the example of love that I aspire to be. She has room enough in her heart for me and the rest of the planet. She is like an incubator of love, growing little souls into the magnificent beings that they are. She is my guiding light, my guardian angel, my teacher, my mentor, my way shower and the love of my life. Ajanel, this book would not have been written were it not for you and my life wouldn't be the fantastic experience it is either. I love you...always and forever.

A FEW THINGS TO REMEMBER TO MAKE YOUR LIFE BETTER RIGHT NOW!

- *Life is like magic. It only looks difficult until you know the secrets.*

- *Deal with a problem at its core and it won't come back anymore.*

- *Being poor is a disease of the mind. You don't want to catch it.*

- *When you change your own mind, the change is permanent.*

- *Obstacles are seen by unsuccessful people on their way to failure.*

- *Trust your gut no matter what and you'll never get stuck in a rut.*

- *Love is an eternally blossoming flower and you are the garden that gives it life.*

- *People say what they say and do what they do. How you react is totally up to you.*

- *You're either 100% committed to success or failure. There is no third option.*

- *Is what you're doing right now bringing you closer to or taking you further from what you're committed to?*

DARSHAN G. SHANTI
"THE 24-HOUR CHAMPION®"

THE IDEAL PROFESSIONAL SPEAKER FOR YOUR NEXT EVENT

• Keynotes • Breakouts • 1/2, Full or Multi-Day Workshops

SOME TALK TOPICS

1. The 24-Hour Champion – Discover And Live Your Priceless Life
2. How To Sell 10x More ...Without Selling
3. The 1 Degree Difference Between Success And Failure
4. Fear No More! – Replacing Fear With Courage
5. How Your Perceptions Create Your Workplace
6. The Turning Point – From Failure and Frustration To Love and Joy
7. Communicating To Win In Every Situation
8. Creating An Atmosphere of Respect In The Workplace
9. Stress No More!
10. Managing Diversity Without Adversity
11. The Possible You – Finding Your Purpose By Finding Yourself
12. Unstoppability – The 5 Key Characteristics of the Outrageously Successful and Wealthy

---

To Schedule Darshan To Speak At Your Next Event
(505) – 321-4914 or email him at:
darshan@the24hourchampion.com

THANK YOU FOR PURCHASING THIS BOOK
HERE'S A GIFT OF SUPPORT

Personal development is extremely rewarding and it can also be very challenging at times. So, in order to help you get the most out of this, it will be very beneficial for you to have ongoing support. It can often make the difference between rapid and permanent success and a slow, arduous failure. So, because you've invested in yourself, in your dreams, in your life, it deserves a reward. Just go to www.the24hourchampion.com and sign up for my free weekly e-newsletter. It's choc-a-bloc full of time-tested, proven (by me and all my clients) straightforward, real-life tools and resources that will support you in living the life you've always wanted and having outrageous success in your business. It will inspire you each week with new ideas, challenge you to break out of your old patterns and most importantly, continue to help you grow.

TABLE OF CONTENTS

FOREWORD xiii

INTRODUCTION. xvii

CHAPTER 1: What You Believe Is What You Get. 1

CHAPTER 2: Forgive And Be Free 23

CHAPTER 3: Taking Total Responsibility And 41
Ownership Of Your Life

CHAPTER 4: Becoming Congruent - A Front 69
And Rear End Alignment

CHAPTER 5: The Power Of Commitment. 89

CHAPTER 6: Trust Your Gut No Matter What 115

CHAPTER 7: Love Is Really All There Is 131

CHAPTER 8: The Art Of Balance 147

CHAPTER 9: Action! Action! Action!. 171

CLOSING THOUGHTS/AFTERWORD 193

ABOUT THE AUTHOR. 195

RESOURCES TO SUPPORT YOU. 197
AFTER READING THE BOOK

HELP CHANGE SOMEONE'S LIFE TODAY
"SHARE THIS BOOK"

The 24-Hour Champion – Discovering And Living Your Priceless Life is a book about you. It's a book about achieving your wants, your needs, your desires, your goals, your dreams and it's about helping you to have that life and have it now.

The exercises in this book will take you on your own personal journey of self-discovery, empowerment and transformation by working with your conscious and unconscious mind and your emotions. Therefore you are not just a passenger along for the ride, but rather the driver of your own personal development. When you change your own mind about who you are and what you want, your life changes immediately and it opens the way for a brand new future.

$19.95

Special Quantity Discounts Purchased Directly From Darshan

        10-20 Books. $17.95

        21-99 Books. $14.95

        100-499 Books. $12.95

        500-999 Books. $10.95

        1,000 + Books $7.95

To Place An Order,
Visit www.the24hourchampion.com or call
(505)- 321-4914

FOREWORD

You hold in your hands a priceless treasure – your future life! This book opens you to your unlimited potential and the unlimited possibilities of your future. DOING this book will make a huge difference in your life; just reading this book will make little difference in your life. *The 24-Hour Champion* spans the range of deep personal development to the practical daily activities of being a champion. The principles presented are congruent with those taught by sages throughout the ages. This book is the vehicle for you to put those principles into practice, rather than simply a presentation of them to you.

The 24-Hour Champion is not a book for the complacent person. It is for a person of courage. The courage to fully engage in the admonition: "Know thyself." The author's directions are clear, succinct and unambiguous; the reader that truly wants to be a 24-hour champion only has to implement them. This is not a theoretical book. It is a book of practical application that is validated by the author's own experience of dedicated self-discovery about why his life was not what he wanted it to be and how he changed it. It is written in clear, straight-forward, simple and honest language.

The author speaks to you personally in a conversational mode and expects your response. This approach guides you on the path that freed him. It employs the most powerful and quickest learning process, the Socratic method, by providing you with vital information and then asking you to respond to questions that relate that information directly to you and your life. The author will not tell you about you; you will tell you about you. Transformation results from your own internal recognition of the points presented through your personal responses. The author then summarizes the most salient points presented to increase your retention of them. While every chapter in this book provides great value to you; the Chapter 8 activities may well be the most valuable in guiding you to being a 24-hour champion, but the other chapters must be completed first.

Working through this book, not just reading it will save you: the hours of reading the same books the author did, the same time and money the author spent on self-improvement programs and the years of unhappiness he endured. *The*

24-Hour Champion uses both positive and negative examples to communicate clearly the points being made. The author illustrates and validates critical points with powerful real life experiences of other individuals as well as those of his own. The author is very open about and shares what he has learned from his life experiences of what did and did not create the life of his desires. He shows by his own history, at the extremes, that transformation is possible so that whether you are living at those extremes or not, you can believe you too can transform.

Consequently, *The 24-Hour Champion* is very UPLIFTING. It is presented from the viewpoint that the reader "does not need to be fixed" but as Michelangelo said of his sculpting: *"I saw the angel in the marble and carved until I set him free. The sculptor's hand can only break the spell to free the figures slumbering in the stone."* With this book you are the sculptor, sculpting your future life by chiseling away the extraneous material your true identity has accumulated in order to bring forth the true you. **This book is your chisel.**

"Chiseling" with *The 24-Hour Champion* will guide you through a process of discovering the fundamental causes that have resulted in the life you have created to date and reveal:

- What is behind your behaviors that have created your life so far
- Why yours and other people's lives are the way they are with clear examples of how those fundamental causes were created
- The reasons those fundamental causes are invalid
- Your limiting paradigm or the unconscious boundaries you place on yourself
- Why changing your life has been difficult, if not impossible to date
- The greatest enemy to being a 24-hour champion is your own ego
- How living from intuition takes stress out of your life and guides you on the shortest and safest path to your life's destination
- Why fear must be cleared first because of what it does to attempt to control situations and block intuition
- Most importantly, the doorway to new and valid causes that will create the limitless life you desire and truly deserve

Through the process, the critical emotions to evoke change will be engaged. You will discover why the work you have done on yourself has not produced all the change you say you want. You will understand that accepting full responsibility for your experiences is empowering, while making others responsible for your experience is giving away your power.

Bluntly you are told you alone are totally accountable and responsible for what results from DOING *The 24-Hour Champion* and that the author has fulfilled his responsibility of providing the vehicle for those results. Consequently this challenges you to do what is necessary to not need another book, seminar or training to live a fulfilling life.

Reader: Can you be as open and free as the author to put on paper your similar most personal experiences? If you will, *The 24-Hour Champion* will be well worth the time you invest in it. If not, and you still want to be free, return to it when you are ready to do so.

This book is not intended for one time use. Its greatest value is that you can reuse it as you grow and continue to become the beautiful and polished being you truly are, just like Michelangelo's finished sculptures.

PERSONAL NOTE: I have known the author for many years and observed his own transformation through his past and continuing use of the processes in *The 24-Hour Champion*. I too have been on the path to discover my true self and studied human behavior and consciousness for over 25 years. In that time I have worked with some of the most effective personal development teachers. None of them have put all of these principles and processes into a single book or experience. Had this book been available and accessible to me when I started on that path, my life would be even more glorious than it is today. – Jim Campbell, President, Wellness Improvement Experts

INTRODUCTION

What does it take to become a champion? Perhaps more importantly, what does it take to be a champion 24-hours a day and what does it take to stay that way? Is that even possible? Realistic? Doable? Most people would think it is not. Most people would be wrong. You see, it all starts with your imagination.

IMAGINE

Imagine for a moment that your life is not what you think it is. Then imagine for a moment that who you really are isn't who you think you are.

If that were true, then what? Who would you be and what would your life look like?

This book is going to help you become an artist, specifically a sculptor. First, you'll look at the artwork you have created and called, "Your Life." You'll see how it has been shaped, formed, put together. You'll see how it has been chipped, hurt and worn away. You'll see how in spite of all that, it has protected itself and survived.

Then as you begin to appreciate more and more your true beauty, The 24- Hour Champion will help you develop fine, artistic sculpting skills. And like Michelangelo, through self-discovery, you will begin to consciously and purposefully mold and create yourself into a beautiful, perfect, finished piece. You will not just be creating artwork anymore; you will be creating a masterpiece.

At that point, you will be free. You'll be free to do what you want to do and live the way you want to live. You will be free from your past blocks, beliefs and barriers and you'll be free to be who you want to be starting right now. And as you show the world this real you, they will ask, "How did he do that? And how come his life is so easy?" And then you can smile inside and quietly say to them, "Imagine for a moment that who you really are is not who you think you are."

THE NEXT STAGE IN YOUR JOURNEY BEGINS HERE

What you are about to discover is the most beautiful thing in the Universe. What you are about to discover is so precious, so priceless, so magnificent, so special, so powerful, so beautiful, so unique, so fabulous and so full of love. What you are about to discover, is you...the real you.

You are a champion, a winner, a gift to the world and it is the purpose of The 24-hour Champion to bring that out of you and to help you realize that and live that way every day... for the rest of your life. Soon you will discover how really, really easy it is to be who you are and how very difficult and painful and stressful it is to be who you are not. I am going to be speaking to you as the magnificent and powerful person you are, not the person, up to this point, you have believed yourself to be.

Changing your life is far easier than you might imagine. It is the resistance to change, the struggle, the fight, the desire to hold on to the old and your fear that causes you to think and to believe it is so difficult.

Here are the steps to realizing the truth of who you are and then living that way. The question is, will you do them?

1. Discover your core, unconscious, negative beliefs and replace them with conscious positive beliefs.
2. Unconditionally and completely forgive yourself and all those around you that you have not forgiven for whatever they did or didn't do.
3. Take full responsibility for **everything** in your life.
4. Look at and list all the areas in which you're incongruent (say one thing but do another).
5. Reexamine all of your commitments. In other words, what are you really committed to in life? Be totally honest.
6. Trust, listen to and follow the wisdom of your intuition.
7. Love yourself, respect yourself, value yourself, appreciate yourself, honor yourself, cherish yourself and live that way from now on without exception.
8. Find balance. Be grateful. Live in the moment.
9. Take laser focused, massive action toward your dreams. Never give up until they're done.

What I have just shared with you is what this book is all about and what it will help you to do. If you do these nine things, you're going to have a magnificent life, outrageous success, off the charts happiness, satisfaction and fulfillment. Don't be like I was. I did some of them. I even mastered some, but I didn't do them all. As a result, I struggled miserably, made myself sick, really sick and suffered for years and years. As bluntly as I can put it, that life was disgustingly horrible. I will never live that way again!

IS THIS BOOK FOR YOU?

This is really a manual for living an amazing life and having an outrageously successful business. Let me be clear right from the start. You are not going to absorb this information through osmosis. You're going to have to be willing to do the work...all the work. There are NO exceptions to this whatsoever. If you're used to taking shortcuts, it won't work here.

Make note of the following bulleted points and adhere to them closely as they will help you to get the highest benefits in your life.

- Decide right now that you are going to change and not let anything stop you
- Believe in yourself and in your future and that you can have what you want
- Do what it says to do in its entirety no matter how uncomfortable it might be
- Keep focused on the end result, not the temporary condition you're in now
- Don't give up
- Be willing to go where you haven't gone and do what you haven't done
- Keep a very open mind

It would be a very good idea for you to read this book over many weeks. In fact, you should read the whole book many times as you enter different stages in your life because as you grow and come to new levels of understanding in life, parts of this book will speak to you differently. For now, taking a chapter a week and really working on it would be a very good idea. That will give you time to incorporate all the ideas. Spaced repetition learning is critical to change lifelong patterns and behaviors. And keep this in mind as well. Studies of learning show that on first exposure, people:

Retain 10% of what they read
Retain 20% of what they hear
Retain 30% of what they see
Retain 50% of what they see & hear
Remember 70% of what they say and
Remember 90% of what they do

This book will involve a great deal of doing.

With that said, <u>The 24-Hour Champion</u> is totally about you. Each word, line, paragraph and chapter is totally written with you in mind. Now, I don't know you and I don't pretend to. So the question arises, how can this book be totally about you? Well the answer to that lies in the fact that you are going to be doing a great deal of self-discovery. Your self-discovery is all about you. This book is all about your self-discovery.

If this is the first book you've ever read to help improve your life, hang on because you're about to go for one heck of a ride and you're going to be transported light years ahead of where you are. If you've read dozens of books and have been doing personal development for a while, then this book will enable you to discover the remaining puzzle pieces that have been missing so that you can put them into place and immediately make your life start to work the way you've always wanted it to.

If you are sick and tired of being sick and tired and you have reached a point where if you don't do something now, you never will, this book is for you. If you're dissatisfied with your life in terms of your relationships, your finances, your health, your happiness, joy, fulfillment or satisfaction, this book is for you. If you are breathing, can read and have any desire for something more out of your life and you are ready, willing and committed to do something about it, then this book is for you.

A word of caution. Please don't put the responsibility of changing your life on this book because this book will **NOT CHANGE YOUR LIFE**. It can't. In fact, nothing outside of you can. Only you can. All this book, or any other book, seminar, workshop, CD program or therapy can do is to bring you to new levels of awareness. That in turn, brings you to a decision point... a new turning point in your life. If you decide not to make the turn, that's on you.

The entire responsibility for changing your life lies in you. Because of that, I make you no promise that if you read it, your relationships will improve, you will find the answers you've been looking for, life will finally make sense, etc., etc. So if I can't promise you that you will get those or any other benefits, why would you read it?

There is no one answer to that. There are many. Somewhere in this book you will discover yourself. Where that will be, I don't know, nor could I pretend to know. What I can promise is that the <u>24-Hour Champion</u> is written in such a way that it would be impossible for you not to discover whatever it is you are looking for.

In order to get the most out of it, you'll have to put the most into it that you can. I can tell you right now, most people won't do that. Most people won't even come close. They won't do the exercises. They won't do the 'work' suggested in the book because it is too much for them or it is too hard or too whatever. One of my colleague's summed it up best when he said, "People want to make changes. They don't want to change." If that's you, just go fishing instead of taking the time to read this. You'll have a lot more fun in the short run.

The point is, you have to really want to do the work on yourself and in your life and you have to believe it is going to work. When you want freedom, joy, peace, happiness, riches, fulfillment, satisfaction, etc., as much as you want the air you're breathing right now, then and only then, will you have it. If it is anything less than that, you will back out and find a way to sabotage yourself and your dreams.

I can and do assure you. IT IS NOT ONLY POSSIBLE, IT IS AN ABSOLUTE FACT that you will have the life of your dreams if you do this work. If it were not a fact, then all the people who have done personal development work would be living lives that are not to their liking. That brings me to a big point. There are people who spend years doing every kind of personal development work they can do. They read every book, go to every seminar, listen to every audio program, yet nothing is different in their lives. They are form without substance. The reason is simple. They have never really done the work, the core work that is necessary. They just scratch the surface and dance around the issues, never going deep enough to get the job done. They refuse to take 100% personal responsibility. Being an insight/awareness/personal growth junkie is very different than being a 24-hour champion.

If you're thinking, "It's not possible for me to live a great life or to truly be happy!" please read no further. You've already stopped all the possibilities from occurring. You've already made up your mind. The fact of the matter is that your life can be whatever you want it to be in the moment you decide for it to be. You have all the power. But if you don't believe that you do have all the power, that's when life doesn't work. That's all about to change.

The following is a brief overview and a list of benefits associated with each chapter. When you read these benefits now, it will set your mind up to be on the lookout for them and will help you to get the most out of this book.

CHAPTER ONE – WHAT YOU BELIEVE IS WHAT YOU GET

We'll examine your core beliefs about your life. This is the most important step as it sets the foundation for all the other steps to build on.

In Chapter One, you'll:
- Discover the core, unconscious, negative beliefs that have held you back in life and how to break free of them FOREVER!
- Learn to replace these self-limiting beliefs with new, deeply anchored, positive beliefs that become the foundation and guiding principals that run your life
- Master a simple tool that you can use for the rest of your life to instantly turn your beliefs around if you ever find yourself stuck
- Increase your confidence and self-esteem, not just incrementally, but exponentially
- Wash away past emotional blocks and pain that have been weighing you down like a pair of lead boots

CHAPTER TWO – FORGIVE AND BE FREE

Forgiveness is the ultimate gift that you give to yourself and those around you. Once you realize how your beliefs were formed and you are consciously living, it will become imperative to master the "heart" of forgiveness.

In Chapter Two, you'll:
- Forgive yourself for anything and everything you've done
- Forgive others for their 'offenses' to you no matter how bad they were
- Free yourself from any resentment, pain, anger or hurt that you're experiencing as a result
- Leave your past where it belongs…in the past and start fresh
- Begin to heal long-time emotional wounds

CHAPTER THREE – TAKING TOTAL OWNERSHIP OF YOUR LIFE

Once you have forgiven yourself and become aware of your unconscious beliefs and they are not in control anymore, you'll learn to be responsible for who you really ARE, instead of who you believed you WERE.

In Chapter Three, you'll:
- Learn to be responsible instead of taking responsibility. This small distinction can mean the difference between success and failure in all areas of your life
- Discover how you can instantly feel happier any time…once and for all
- Gain boundless energy when you stop carrying the weight of the world on your shoulders
- Begin to put yourself first and start being responsible for you
- Learn to effectively make decisions…and to be confident in the decisions you make

CHAPTER FOUR – BECOMING CONGRUENT - A FRONT AND REAR END ALIGNMENT

Who you say you are and what you do need to be in alignment. If they are not, life becomes a struggle, confusing, much harder and business suffers.

In Chapter Four, you'll:
- Experience a tremendous peace of mind and calmness that you never thought possible
- Improve your relationships with friends, family and with yourself
- Experience more harmony in your business and life
- Learn to make subtle, yet profound changes that will cause people to trust you more and to want to do business with you
- Get to the core of what stops you and transform it once and for all

CHAPTER FIVE - THE POWER OF COMMITMENT

Without commitment, you will back out of your promises. Commitments shouldn't imprison you…nor should you be afraid of them or their consequences.

In Chapter Five, you'll:
- Discover the negative and positive commitments you've made with yourself in the past
- Use commitments to drive you forward, not hold you back
- Improve your performance and increase your productivity in your business and your life
- Free yourself from past commitments that no longer serve you
- End procrastination forever…and have much more free time

CHAPTER SIX – TRUST YOUR GUT NO MATTER WHAT

Learn to use the power of the Universe for ultimate success. Your intuition will never lead you astray and will always make your life better.

In Chapter Six, you'll:

- Discover how to attract the people and the circumstances that you need to succeed
- Learn how to make your life flow easier/smoother in virtually every area
- Discover ways to attract the future of your business and life rather than forcing it
- Be able to trust yourself and the Universe more
- Allow the power of faith (believing in the unseen) to work its magic

CHAPTER SEVEN – LOVE IS REALLY ALL THERE IS

Develop a sense of peace, harmony, joy, happiness and satisfaction. Then live from that place on a regular basis. Learn to let go of the pain, fear, stress, anxiety, overwhelm and uncertainty that plague you. Then learn to live as love.

In Chapter Seven, you'll:

- Open your heart to the miracle that love is
- Learn to love yourself and others unconditionally
- Discover the incredible healing power of love
- Be able to let go of past resentments and anger

CHAPTER EIGHT – THE BALANCE OF BALANCE

This is an extra important chapter because you will be putting your entire life together so that it all balances out. When you're out of balance, things get all messed up...and beyond the stress, anxiety, guilt and pain it causes, this is when physical problems start to manifest.

In Chapter Eight, you'll:

- Find ways to create more stability in your life and business
- Discover your core values which will guide your every decision
- Discover ways to feel healthier and more "alive"
- Learn to enjoy your life and business more
- Establish your top three to five priorities
- Learn how to set proper boundaries

CHAPTER 9 –ACTION, ACTION, ACTION

With the past eight steps in place, you can take appropriate, massive, laser-focused action. Without action, nothing matters and nothing happens. This chapter is all about putting into action everything that you've been working on over the past eight chapters.

In Chapter 9, you'll:
• Begin to think like a wealthy person
• Understand how to easily write and achieve your goals
• Develop a solid action plan to take your goals and launch them immediately
• Learn the simplest priority management system on the planet
• Become much more productive and much less busy

IT'S TIME TO BEGIN

Answer the following questions as thoroughly as possible.

1. **Are you ready to have an absolutely amazing life?** Yes or No? _____

2. **Describe what an amazing life is for you.** Be specific. Where would you live? What would you do for a career? How much money would you make? How would you feel on a daily basis? Etc.

    _____

    _____

    _____

    _____

3. **Assuming your answer is a resounding YES, please explain why you're ready.** Really feel what you are writing. If you just put down surface level answers like, "Because it's time." Or, "I'm not getting any younger." those reasons won't be strong enough motivators. You must truly feel the hunger deep down inside and experience a burning desire to change. Your emotions are the key. Feel this out. Listen to your heart as you write your answer.

    _____

    _____

    _____

    _____

Then ask yourself what you would like to get out of reading this book. In other words, what do you really, really want for your life? Do not let yourself get away with saying, "I don't know!" It's just a cop out, an excuse that your unconscious mind uses to keep you stuck.

4. **Just list what you want.** I'm not asking you to believe you can have it yet, so don't censor your list

    _____

    _____

_____

_____

5. **Why do you want what you just wrote?** This is vitally important. Knowing why is like the fuel that will transport your dreams into realities. Knowing why will be the stimulus, the motivation, the energy that keeps you going even when the going is tough.

_____

_____

_____

_____

6. **What are you going to do to ensure that you get what you say you want?** Since neither this book, nor I can do it for you, you need to be clear about what you are going to do. If your intention is just to read the pages but not do the "work", I would suggest you file it away until you are willing to do the work. It will be here when you are ready.

_____

_____

_____

_____

You are now set to get the most out of The <u>24-Hour Champion</u> that you possibly can. To complete this introduction, here's a quote from Krishnamurti (1984 UN Peace Medal Winner). I suggest you follow his advice to the letter.

"What we are about to undertake is an expedition together, a journey of discovery into the most secret recesses of our consciousness… forget everything you know about yourself: forget everything that you have thought about yourself; we are going to set off as if we know nothing."

"I can't teach anyone, anything.
I can only make them think."

Socrates

CHAPTER 1

WHAT YOU BELIEVE IS WHAT YOU GET

"As you think, so shall you be." – Dr. Wayne Dyer

One of the first things you need to do to realize the champion within is to establish a baseline understanding of where you are right now. The reason for this is simple. If you don't know where you're starting from, you won't know how to reach your goal. In other words, if you want to go to California, but you don't know your starting point, how can you plan your direction? It's impossible.

I have created a survey for you to take that will help you to establish your own baseline about where you are right now in terms of how you feel about yourself and your life. Before you take it, make sure you read the directions very carefully and you follow them to the letter.

LIFE SATISFACTION SURVEY

The following survey has the power to change your life if it is done the way it is meant to be done. The challenge with it is that your unconscious beliefs and fears may prevent you from rating yourself accurately. This explanation will help you to bypass the pitfalls and get the most out of this that you possibly can.

Take your finances for example. Let's say you make $50,000 a year and that's good to you. So, you rate yourself an 8. You may think, "If I was making $100,000 a year, then I would rate that area as a 10." In reality, if nothing was stopping you from making all the money you want, you probably would not have rated yourself that high. In fact, $50,000 would barely have rated a 1.

The reason is that your ego doesn't want you to believe you're capable of making much more money than that because it wants to keep you from failing and experiencing any kind of pain. It will also try to fool you into thinking that the amount you currently make is all you really "should" have because you don't "need" anymore.

Since your ego's job is to protect you from pain, and failure is pain, it gives you a false sense of security to keep you from thinking that you're failing. It also protects you from being uncomfortable. If you were to do everything it took to make that kind of money, it would mean you would have to leave your comfort zone and let go of the life you're familiar with living. Your ego wants you to believe that all those changes would be too 'painful', so it doesn't want you to go there and throws up every kind of smoke screen it can.

With that in mind, as you rate yourself in each of the following areas, DREAM BIG. Know that failure isn't an option. Believe that whatever you want, you can have.

So, if you're making $50,000 a year and want to make $50 million, how would you rate yourself then? If your relationship is the best it has ever been, but a far cry from where it could be, how would you rate that? It is the same with your career and all other areas of the survey.

One last thing. Your ego may start to attack this survey by saying something like, "Life can never be that good. It's a waste of time trying. Don't bother with this. You've got more important things to do."

If that happens, IGNORE IT AT ALL COSTS. If you listen to your ego, you won't have the life of your dreams.

YOU DESERVE
THE LIFE OF YOUR DREAMS!

INSTRUCTIONS FOR THE LIFE SATISFACTION SURVEY

Honestly rate yourself on a scale of 1 to 10. A 1 means this is an area that needs much improvement and a rating of 10 means that you're totally satisfied with where you are in your life.

Keep this in mind as you rate yourself. This is NOT an improvement scale. So, if you would rank yourself higher now than you would have some time in the past, that doesn't apply to this survey. This survey is only interested in where you are now compared to where you really, really want to be. The more truthful you are, the better.

1. My Overall Life Satisfaction/Fulfillment   1 2 3 4 5 6 7 8 9 10

2. My Financial Success   1 2 3 4 5 6 7 8 9 10

3. My Relationship With My Partner   1 2 3 4 5 6 7 8 9 10

4. My Other Relationships   1 2 3 4 5 6 7 8 9 10

5. My Career Satisfaction And Success   1 2 3 4 5 6 7 8 9 10

6. My Self-Value   1 2 3 4 5 6 7 8 9 10

7. My Level of Happiness/Joy   1 2 3 4 5 6 7 8 9 10

8. My Passion For Life   1 2 3 4 5 6 7 8 9 10

9. My Freedom To Be Myself   1 2 3 4 5 6 7 8 9 10

10. My Purpose In Life   1 2 3 4 5 6 7 8 9 10

11. My Self-Approval   1 2 3 4 5 6 7 8 9 10

12. My Personal Power   1 2 3 4 5 6 7 8 9 10

13. My Balance In All Life Areas   1 2 3 4 5 6 7 8 9 10

14. My Spirituality   1 2 3 4 5 6 7 8 9 10

15. My Physical Well Being   1 2 3 4 5 6 7 8 9 10

16. My Hopes/Dreams And Goals   1 2 3 4 5 6 7 8 9 10

17. My Courage   1 2 3 4 5 6 7 8 9 10

18. My Ease Of Life   1 2 3 4 5 6 7 8 9 10

19. The Love That I Feel/Experience   1 2 3 4 5 6 7 8 9 10

20. My Fun/Play/Excitement   1 2 3 4 5 6 7 8 9 10

OK, well what did you discover? Did you rank yourself higher, lower or about where you believed you should have been? If you circled mostly low numbers, what does that tell you? If you were in the middle for most of your answers, that means you're living a mediocre life. There's so much more to life than just being average. If most of your answers were on the high end, perhaps you don't need this book at this time. If that's the case, congratulations. Please share it with someone else.

What I can tell you is that I have given this survey out to countless numbers of people and some of them had lives that were in shambles, but they rated themselves as very high in most every area. I've also had people who circled all ones. I've had some people draw an arrow to the left of # 1 on each one. Once again, your ego will do what it can to keep you where you are. Don't worry. By the time you're done with this book, your ego won't have the control over you that it has now.

Yet it doesn't really matter where you are right now. What I mean by that is that you shouldn't add any significant meaning to the fact that your life isn't where you want it to be. In fact, do the opposite. Use this information as a springboard to launch your life from. The real significance for doing the survey is that you now have a starting point from which you can work from. After all, you didn't buy this book to stay where you are, did you? No, you bought it because you want to be somewhere different than you are now. So, if you circled a 4 on question 7 (Your level of happiness and joy) and you want to be a 10, then everything that is in this book is to help you get to that level. In any event, now that you have a baseline, you can work more effectively and much more quickly at getting what you want out of life. So let's start by looking at your beliefs.

Your Beliefs Become Your Reality...
Period. End Of Story

Have you ever wondered how some people have so much and others have so little? Have you ever wondered why some people who have every adversity imaginable can overcome those adversities and thrive? Have you ever wondered how some people with very little to no education become multi-millionaires and people with PhD's are just getting by? Have you ever seen a family in which one sibling does extremely well and the other doesn't?

What is the difference between people who have phenomenal success and those who don't? What is happening in their thoughts and beliefs that cause them to live lives they truly enjoy, while others never break the chain of struggle, fear, pain and despair?

In truth, that's a loaded question. On the surface, it looks like there would be many, many factors because there are so many people, so many personalities, so many different circumstances, etc. But it's all rooted in the same thing.

At the core of all human behavior are unconscious/subconscious beliefs. In other words, what controls behavior in people are the things they are completely unaware of, blind spots if you will.

Dr. Phil calls these beliefs, 'tapes'. He says,

> Tapes are long-held, lightening fast, automatic thoughts that program you for a specific outcome, oftentimes without you being aware of it. They are a natural and uncontrollable reflex and work as independently as your organs. Unfortunately, this means that your tapes can control your every move and make you a mere passenger in your own life. These powerful thoughts may actually program you to behave in ways you don't want to.

I take that one step further. Those thoughts and beliefs DO PROGRAM YOU to behave in ways you DON'T WANT TO. There are no ifs, ands or buts about it. Worse yet, you are powerless to change them because it is not what you know about your life that runs it. It is what you don't know. And the fact of the matter is, YOU CAN'T CHANGE WHAT YOU DON'T KNOW...EVER.

Your unconscious perceptions, thoughts, beliefs, etc. are truly blind spots and are what cause you to repeat over and over again what you don't want to do but are helpless to stop. In other words, your unconscious thoughts are running your life and until they become conscious, you will stay stuck.

If you think of a side-view mirror in a car, that will illustrate the point exactly. Let's say you're driving down the highway and you want to change lanes. You look in your side-view mirror and don't see anything. So, you proceed to change lanes. Next thing you know, you're being honked at, or you are in an accident. Why? You looked and no one was there. You could not see the other driver. So based on what you saw (and did not see) you made a judgment and took action on that judgment. Your blind spots (things you are not conscious of and can not see) can be dangerous because they will allow you to have a false sense of security and cause you to do things that you would not have done if you were aware of them. That information is all well and good. But just understanding that concept will make very little, if any difference to you. So, what we are going to do in this chapter is to help you discover your unconscious beliefs that you formed many years ago so that you can take back control of your life and start consciously directing it where you want it to go.

Some of what you're about to discover will be very insightful and you may experience a great deal of relief from some long-held issues immediately. Some of it may be quite humorous. In fact, it's a good idea to keep your sense of humor as you go through this process. In other words, don't take it so seriously that you debilitate yourself. With that said, some of what you're about to discover may be very difficult to look at and to deal with. It may be quite painful in some cases. You may have many thoughts telling you to not do the work, telling you it's not worth it, telling you to put it off until later, telling you that this stuff is not necessary and that you'll be fine without it.

DON'T LISTEN!

If you do, you'll be putting off the happiness, joy, freedom, satisfaction, fulfillment and love that will be yours in the moment you deal with the unconscious beliefs that are stopping you. The key is to keep focusing on where you're going, not where you've been or where you are currently, no matter how bad you think it is. Also, keep focusing on what you want, not what you don't. And keep focusing on the pleasure and benefits and the rewards.

You Never Go For Things
You Don't Believe You Can Achieve

Your life is a product of your beliefs. What you believe about the world is how it will always be. What you believe the most strongly about yourself will always come true. As this chapter suggests, what you believe is what you get. What you think about, you bring about. Your thoughts create your reality. As a man thinketh in his heart, so is he. It doesn't matter how it is said or in how many ways, it's all boils down to the same thing. Your life is a product of what you constantly think about whether you're conscious of those thoughts or not.

Your beliefs are formed early in your childhood, usually under the age of seven when your mind is primarily in the Theta state. The Theta state is almost like a hypnotic state. When you're in it, you are very open to suggestion. I am not going to get any more technical than that. It's unimportant. What is important is that you understand that it is natural that a young child would spend a great deal of time there because he is learning so much. In fact, his very survival depends on it.

So, when events happen, if there is a ton of repetition associated with it, it programs you to start thinking and believing that way. On top of that, if there is a huge emotional impact, it goes right to the unconscious and permanently parks itself there. As a result, it is vital to revisit those early years of your life when you were most impressionable, when you were learning how the world works, how you fit in and how best you were going to make it through.

So in order to change your life, you will need to see how you put it together. Once you see how you have created your life, then you can take it apart, get rid of the 'building blocks' you don't want or need anymore and replace them with better, healthier, more stable material.

You are now going to look at how you developed your identity. What you will also see is how your identity developed you. Like habits, first you develop them and then they develop you and keep you doing the same thing over and over and over.

I am now going to take you through a step by step process that will help you put the entire picture of your life together. It will help you fill in all the blanks that might have been missing for you. You will probably get many "A-Ha" moments. Things in your life that have never made any sense will suddenly begin to. You'll stop repeating negative, self-defeating patterns. You'll become energized, more motivated and more inspired. In short, once you see how you've put the entire picture of your life together, you'll be free. You'll be free from the negative and you'll be free to be who you really want to be. So let's get started.

How You Developed Your Identity

There are ten steps in this process to help you discover how you got to be who you are right now. We'll go through each one and discuss it. Except for steps 8 and 9, there will be things for you to think about and then write down. Also, each of the numbered items are written in 'I' language so that when you read it, it is more personal and will have a deeper meaning to you. I am going to list all ten first and then break each one of them down separately.

1. The **ORIGINATING EVENT** - I see something, hear something, experience something, etc. For example, my father says to me, "You'll never amount to anything!"

2. **THE PERCEPTION** – I have a perception of those words. I may be "shocked" because I had always been told how "adorable, cute and cuddly" I was and this is like a slap in the face.

3. **THE THOUGHTS** – I now have thoughts (unconscious and conscious) about that perception, not the event itself, but my perception of the event. I may think something like, "He's right!" The fact of the matter is that as a 5-year-old, I would have to accept what he says as 100% truth. There is no other decision I could make because I don't have the reasoning ability or the capacity to think otherwise.

4. **THE EMOTIONS** – Next, I have emotions caused by those thoughts. The emotions must always be consistent with the thoughts. In other words, I can't have an emotion that is not consistent with the thought. That is the way it is.

5. **THE SURVIVAL DECISION** – I make a decision(s) based on my perception, thoughts and feelings about myself, others and the world around me. These decisions help me to get by, to make it and survive in the world. Usually the decision is negative. I may decide something like, "I am not good enough." or "I am worthless." This is my *survival decision*. It is my unconscious way of being that is always running in the background of everything I do, think and say. It literally dictates what I do and don't do and I am completely unaware of it. In effect, it is the strings that are pulling me and clouds all my future perceptions, judgments and decisions.

The reason it's called a survival decision is that it is designed to keep you in survival (your lungs taking in air and your heart beating) and nothing more. Survival is just existence. Your ego's job is to maintain that existence. More on the ego's job later.

6. **THE TESTING STAGE** - I actively seek other people to agree with my decision. I begin to search for evidence and I keep searching and I keep finding the evidence to validate or to invalidate my thoughts.

7. THE BELIEF(S) - My thoughts and feelings turn into something stronger, thicker and more solid. I am less flexible and open.

8. TIME PASSES - I keep finding more evidence to back up my decision. I keep having more thoughts and feelings and repeated experiences. This can take place over several days, several weeks, several months or over several years. In effect, I influence myself and really begin to tune out what is going on around me and am only seeing what I want to see, hearing what I want to hear, believing what I want to believe, not what is actually happening. So, if I really believe I am worthless, then even if people tell me that isn't true or if they tell me the complete opposite, I won't be able to hear it.

9. THE KNOWING – Then I know that I am the way I believe I am. At that point it becomes quite hard to change my mind. This works very much against me when it comes to me and what I can do. This is because if I know for sure I can't do something (whether in reality I could or not), I won't do it. This is also true for all relationships. In other words, if I KNOW someone, I can only perceive him or her that way. Therefore, I can't see anything he or she does outside of that perception. In addition, If I KNOW who I am, then nobody will be able to change my mind because I can't separate who I know myself to be from the actual reality. This is my paradigm that prevents me from changing and locks me in and keeps me going down a one way street. I am now blinded by that paradigm and I can't even see the signs that are telling me I am going the wrong way.

10. MY IDENTITY - I now live my life based on the previous nine steps. I am a perfectionist; I am lazy; I am stupid; I am not good enough; I am worthless; I am a failure; I am unlovable; I am wrong; I am unnecessary; I am unredeemable; I don't deserve to live; Men will always leave; Life is hard; Money is bad, etc., etc. In other words, my survival decision is now set in stone. It is tried and true. At this point, it is all unconscious and I unconsciously live my life from this place.

Tonya's Identity Developing Story

I will take you through the ten steps to developing your identity by sharing with you how a past client named Tonya developed her identity. Tonya is a beautiful woman inside and out. She is choc-a-bloc full of love and tenderness, kindness and caring. She has an amazing gift to heal people through her touch. She is extremely intelligent and is a difference maker in the lives of so many people. She is fun, playful and has one of the greatest laughs you will ever hear in your life. She is outgoing, gregarious, playful and quite fun. Oh! (She'd kill me if I didn't put this in here) She's a fabulous cook as well.

But she was also terrified of life. She picked horrible relationships in which she was abused physically, mentally and emotionally. She was powerless and helpless. She was a rescuer. She was a pleaser. She looked (to all outward appearances) very good while believing on the inside that she was really bad. She was a pretender, a phony, a fake. She was living a lie. Her life was held together by a thin veil of false pretenses. She was a master manipulator, a professional victim and she had an excuse for all her failures. I asked Tonya's permission to share her story in the book. She agreed and when I read it to her, she sighed. As if to say, Good Riddance! I don't need that stuff anymore. So here's how she developed her identity.

1. *The Originating Event* - When Tonya was three years old, her Grandmother was painting the back patio to get it ready for a wedding. Tonya wanted to be helpful. She took some paint from the back patio and started to paint her Grandmother's new, white Chevrolet Impala that had just been detailed for the wedding. Her Grandmother beat her severely for that. If that wasn't bad enough for Tonya, when her Grandmother punished Tonya any time after that, she would then feel massively guilty and take Tonya out and buy her a lot of presents. That cycle of punishment and reward repeated itself all throughout Tonya's childhood.

2. Her *perceptions* were shock and confusion and hurt and pain. She (of course) immediately questioned what happened saying, "What did I do?"

3. Her *thoughts* were, "I didn't do anything wrong. I was just trying to help. Why am I in trouble?" And they go even deeper than that. She started to think that she must have been a really bad person. She started to think that she was wrong and unlovable. She began to think she was worthless (worth less). But in addition, **she began associating being punished, being wrong and being bad with love and being loved.** So, in order for her to get anything good, she had to first suffer for it. Unconsciously her thoughts became, "Love has to hurt. Life has to be hard. I need to suffer." In other words, she had to rearrange the events to make it all about her being bad and wrong. So she went from being helpful and good and a

great granddaughter in her own mind, to being bad. It was a natural progression for Tonya to keep thinking that way because her grandmother had to know better than Tonya did. After all, she'd been around a great deal longer.

4. Her *emotions* were - Hurt, devastation and tremendous pain. She felt powerless and helpless. Those are naturally understandable given what she was thinking. Once again, it was her thinking that caused her emotions. And her thinking stemmed from her perception of what happened and everything else had been based from that.

5. Her *survival decision* was – **I AM WRONG**. She developed that decision because she reasoned that by being helpful, she was punished. If you think about the life of someone who is wrong, you can imagine how problematic it is. No matter what she did or didn't do, it was wrong because she was wrong. She spent years and years trying to fix herself, but nothing ever worked because she never got to her core belief. Being wrong was pulling her strings. So everything she did was working within the framework of "Wrong." That meant that even if she did something right, it was 'wrong'. It was a complete lose, lose proposition.

6. Her *testing stage* – Tonya now begins to test her survival decision. She wants to be sure it is going to do the job (keeping her alive). If it doesn't do the job, she would find something that would. So she goes on a proverbial hunt and she finds proof and more evidence from the fact that she had problems with friends all her life; she didn't get along with her family; she had poor relationships; her life was a struggle, constantly full of pain and hurt.

When I said to her, "You are pain and hurt waiting to happen." every light bulb went off in her head. Suddenly her life's struggles all seemed to make sense. She saw how she had been unconsciously creating all of her pain and failure because of her association with receiving good things only after she suffered. She had been living in that unconscious state for about forty-five years continually testing it and it kept working to keep her surviving…but little else. Therefore, she had no incentive to change. She falsely believed that she couldn't be rewarded and loved for being good, so any other model of living wouldn't make sense.

7. Her *belief* about herself was that 'being wrong' was the correct way to live her life. By correct, I mean the best way to survive.

8. *Time passed* – She kept finding more evidence to back up her thoughts and her survival decision and her belief about herself and how to live. As a result, she kept having more problems with friends, family, finances and relationships.

9. *She knew* – Her identity was very well formed. All her walls were put up. Her survival mechanisms were in place.

10. *Her identity* – "I am wrong and I have to suffer to get anything good." That was now an absolute tested, tested and retested fact. All of this occurred while she was still in her early childhood.

OK, now it's your turn. Here are the steps broken down so that you can take yourself through the process.

1. THE ORIGINATING EVENT - I see something, hear something, experience something, etc. For example, my father says to me, "You'll never amount to anything!"

Begin to think about your earliest childhood memories. Some of them were very 'good' and some were 'not so good'. Usually there is some kind of 'traumatic' event that happened to you before the age of seven. Good, not so good and traumatic are in quotes because there are things that happen to us that we label as traumatic and we hold them in our consciousness that way. In reality, they may have been very minor, but to you they may not have been. So do your best to pick a time in your life when you were anywhere from three to seven years old. Maybe you got punished for something you didn't do. Maybe you were trying to be helpful and got in trouble for that. Maybe you brought home straight A's with only one B and got yelled at because they weren't all A's.

So, what is your earliest childhood negative memory or memories? Just list the event or events. Don't write down any of your thoughts or feelings. This negative memory(s) should be pretty clear to you because you've probably told your story of how your sibling was treated much better than you (or something to that effect) many times.

_____

_____

_____

_____

_____

_____

2. THE PERCEPTION – I have a perception of those words. I may be "shocked" because I had always been told how "adorable", "cute" and "cuddly" I was and this is like a slap in the face.

Changing your perceptions is critical to changing your life. Perceptions are first impressions, snap judgments of what is happening. You come up with them instantaneously. They come in so quick that you actually begin to think that what you have perceived about a situation is the same thing as the situation. But of course it's not. What you perceive is what you perceive. What is happening is what is happening. The two are mutually exclusive. Your perceptions are just electrochemical processes happening in your brain. Those electrochemical processes are not the same thing as the actual reality that is occurring. Yet, people will swear up and down that what they perceive is the same thing as what is.

Just think of the last movie you saw with a friend and one of you hated it and one of you loved it. Whose perception was correct? Neither. The movie was the movie. What you and your friend think about the movie is not the movie.

The important part for you to understand is this. Your perception of the outside world is not the outside world. Your perceptions of your friends are not your friends. Your perception of your boss, coworkers and employees are not them as well. Taking it further, your perception of your family is not your family. Yes, that includes your parents and your in-laws. And most importantly, your perception of yourself is not you.

If you have a low opinion of yourself, that's not you. If you have negative beliefs about your life, that's not your life. If you think you'll never amount to anything, it's not true. Contrary to your beliefs about yourself, no matter how true you think they are and no matter how long you've believed in them and no matter the evidence or proof you have as to their validity, they simply are lies, untruths and misconceptions that were based in false associations from your childhood. Get that now and you'll save yourself years of problems, pain, stress and so much more.

Now here is your chance to write down how you interpreted what happened to you. Write down your perceptions (first impressions) of the event(s) you wrote in question number 1.

_____

_____

_____

_____

_____

_____

3. THE THOUGHTS – I now have thoughts (unconscious and conscious) about
that perception, not the event itself, but my perception of the event. I may
think something like, "He's right!" The fact of the matter is that as a 5-year-
old, I would have to accept what he says as 100% truth. There is no other
decision I could make because I don't have the reasoning ability or the capacity to think otherwise.

The things you think about yourself, your parents, your world, literally
begin to create your personality. If as a child you don't feel safe, you'll carry that
with you into adulthood. It will manifest in you not taking risks and instead,
taking the slow and steady approach. Those thoughts just exist in the background and they become your puppeteer. They pull your strings and you can't
stop it. In fact, you don't even know your strings are being pulled. That is what
makes it so difficult to change your life because you don't even know there's a
problem. Even when you do know something is wrong and you want to change
it, the last place you look at is yourself. Why would you when you don't even
know that your strings are being pulled or that anything is wrong? In addition,
it is painful to look at yourself. It is much easier to blame other people than to
take personal responsibility by taking an honest look inside yourself.

So, when you falsely reason that they are "right" about whatever they said
or did to you, then it automatically makes you "wrong." The reason that they
have to be right is simple. If they are wrong, then they can't protect you and you
are in danger...that is, you may be deeply hurt or worse yet, not survive. So this
is a critical part of the development of your identity because your safety, your
security, your survival is paramount as a child; therefore, you are literally depending on whoever is taking care of you for those things. They are your safety,
your security and your survival providers.

You may start to have thoughts like, "Who will take care of me?" "Who
will save me if they can't?" So, without you knowing it, you automatically accept what they say to you and what you say to yourself. From that point on, it
IS YOU.

So write down all the thoughts that you can about the *originating event*.
What did you tell yourself about you? What did you tell yourself about your
future? What did you tell yourself?

_____

_____

_____

_____

4. THE EMOTIONS – Next, I have emotions caused by those thoughts. The emotions must always be consistent with my thoughts. In other words, I can't have an emotion that is not consistent with my thought. That is the way it is.

Your emotions are absolutely vital in the development of your identity because they are like your guidance system. You have 50 to 60 thousand thoughts a day that go through your head and there is no way to monitor them all. However, your emotions come as a result of many, many thoughts. When you're feeling a certain way, it's because you've been thinking a certain way. For example, if you are feeling extremely upset, anxious and afraid because you can't pay your bills, your thoughts would be something like, "How am I going to make it? Is my car going to get repossessed? Where is my money coming from? What am I going to do?"

So if you don't like the way your life is going, begin to monitor your emotions. As you get more and more in tune with yourself, it will be easier for you to change how you feel.

When you write down your emotions, do yourself the favor and really feel them as deeply as you possibly can. Don't worry if you're angry, afraid or very sad. You must feel these emotions to gain leverage on them. If you keep avoiding them, they will always be in control. That is why what you resist, persists. When you own them, they won't own you anymore. When you don't run from them, they won't run you.

So, what are your emotions about each event? _____

_____

_____

_____

5. THE SURVIVAL DECISION – I make a decision(s) based on my perception, thoughts and feelings about myself, others and the world around me. These decisions help me to get by, to make it and survive in the world. Usually the decision is negative. I may decide something like, I am not good enough or I am worthless. This is my *survival decision*. It is the unconscious way of being that is always running in the background of everything I do, think and say. It literally dictates what I do and don't do and I am completely unaware of it. In effect, it is the strings that are pulling me and clouds all my future perceptions, judgments and decisions.

The reason it's called a survival decision is that it is designed to keep you in survival (your lungs taking in air and your heart beating) and nothing more. Survival is just existence. Your ego's job is to maintain that existence.

We will be discussing *decisions* in detail and how powerful they are in chapter three. But for now, just understand that all decisions are made to help you to avoid pain or to gain pleasure.

Your survival decision is a single decision that you make about yourself that literally locks in a set pattern of thinking and feeling from that moment on. It is the foundation of your life. Many decisions will be affected by your survival decision even though you may not even know you made the decision and you don't even know you think that way.

It's like an elephant that is trained from a very young age. The trainers attach its leg to a very, very strong chain. Try as it may, the elephant can't break the chain no matter how it struggles. This fulfills the trainer's purpose. It breaks the elephants will. As it gets older, the chain that is put on the elephant's leg is less and less strong. Eventually it is just a rope that holds the full grown elephant in place. The elephant could easily rip the rope apart and break free just as easily as you could snap a twig. So why doesn't it? It can't because it made a decision that it can't. And it believes its own decision. The elephant programmed itself to stay stuck. The elephant reasoned that it couldn't break free, so it gave up the struggle. It wasn't worth the pain or the effort. It was futile. The elephant believed that he would never break the rope, that it was useless, that he was too weak. And that decision kept him trapped.

But it did other things as well. It kept him from being free. It also kept him from taking risks. It kept him from experiencing the pain of failure. The interesting thing about that was that giving up became the elephant's payoff and it even became comforting. **When giving up became more pleasurable, the elephant had no chance and would never be able change.** Can you see the false connection that the elephant made? Can you see why the elephant made that decision?

It is the same for you. Whatever decision you made was the formation of your identity. When you write your survival decision, keep in mind that it's always about you. So keep peeling layer after layer away and eventually you will get to the core belief, the one that sponsored every other one. The minute you distinguish that decision for yourself, you will begin to put a great deal of things together in your life. You will begin to gain leverage over your past. You'll take a giant leap forward.

List your survival decision here.

_____

6. THE TESTING STAGE - I actively seek other people to agree with my decision. I begin to search for evidence. The problem is that it is all based on my perception. As I just learned, my perception is just an interpretation of what happened and nothing more.

As a child when your identity is being formed, you want to make sure it is going to work to get you by (keep you surviving). So you begin to test your survival decision. So if your survival decision is "I'm a failure," you'll test that. You'll start to do poorly in school. You'll start to get in trouble. You'll start to do things that don't seem to make sense. The reason that happens is that when you think your perception is the way something is (the truth) you want to be validated and justified and so you seek others' validation and approval. In other words, you are now seeking out "proof" that who you say you are is true even if who you say you are is a failure.

Do you truly understand how profound that is? This is like the thick metal chain holding the elephant's leg. You're testing and testing and testing the chain and no matter what, it's not breaking. You keep testing failure in as many ways as you can to make sure it works well. You need to fail so that you can survive. That's what's so insidious, so twisted and so problematic. Said another way, if you change your life by changing your survival mechanisms, that threatens your survival. No one wants their survival threatened, so they stay where they are.

I can't stress the following point enough. Take this to heart and your life will begin to change immediately.

YOU HAVE TO GIVE UP SURVIVING SO THAT YOU CAN LIVE. You can't hold onto the past and have a brand new life and new future. You can't keep doing things the way you've done them and expect your life to be different. And you can't focus on the negative and expect to have positive results.

Now it's your turn. List your *evidence* here that proves your survival decision about yourself is accurate. Just think of the things you did over and over that were to your detriment. Think of the things that people kept telling you to stop doing, but you didn't follow their directions. _____

_____
_____
_____
_____

7. THE BELIEF(S) - My thoughts and feelings turn into something stronger, thicker and more solid. I am less flexible and open.

After the millions of thoughts you've had and all the testing you've done, you really begin to believe that your survival decision is going to work; that is, it is going to keep you alive. As a result, you believe that what you've told yourself is true. At this stage of the game though, there is still room for you to change your mind. Your identity is not set in stone yet.

List any self-limiting beliefs you have.

_____

_____

_____

_____

_____

8. TIME PASSES - I keep finding more evidence to back up my decision. I keep having more thoughts and feelings and repeated experiences. This can take place over several days, several weeks, several months or over several years. In effect, I influence myself and really begin to tune out what is going on around me and am only seeing what I want to see, hearing what I want to hear, believing what I want to believe, not what is actually happening. So, if I really believe I am worthless, then even if people tell me that isn't true, I won't be able to hear it.

Now after millions and millions of more thoughts and feelings, you're pretty sure that your survival decision is right. At this point, you only have a thin chain on your leg and occasionally you may test to see if it will still hold you. Inevitably it will.

9. THE KNOWING – Then I know that I am the way I believe I am. At that point it is quite hard to change my mind. This works very much against me because if I know for sure I can't do something (whether in reality I could or not), I won't do it. This is also true for all relationships. In other words, if I KNOW someone, I can only perceive him or her that way. Therefore, I can't see anything he or she does outside of that perception. In addition, If I KNOW who I am, then nobody will be able to change my mind because

I can't separate who I know myself to be from the actual reality. This is my paradigm that prevents me from changing and locks me in and keeps me going down a one way street. I am now blinded by that paradigm (what I know) and I can't even see the signs that are telling me I am going the wrong way.

At this point, you've tested and retested your theories about yourself and the world. You're now really sure. You have tons of evidence that you're going to survive. You've done it. Now all that you have holding you is a tiny rope, but it doesn't matter because you won't even try to pull it anymore. In fact, you won't even come close to stretching it. There's no need to.

10. MY IDENTITY - I now live my life based on the previous nine steps. I am a perfectionist; I am lazy; I am stupid; I am not good enough; I am worthless; I am a failure; I am unlovable; I am wrong; I am unnecessary; I am unredeemable; I don't deserve to live; Men will always leave; Life is hard; Money is bad, etc., etc. In other words, your survival decision is now set in stone. It is tried and true. It is the way it is and you are the way you are. At this point, it is all unconscious and I unconsciously live my life from this place.

List your identity. I am _____

That's how you got to be the person you are right now. Then based on this model which gets "hardwired" into your brain, you begin to operate that way unconsciously over and over and over FOR THE REST OF YOUR LIFE UNLESS YOU DO SOMETHING TO STOP IT.

Now you know why things never seem to change. You haven't changed. Think of it this way. If you use the same recipe over and over again, you'll always end up with the same result. Your identity is your recipe for survival. It will do anything to stay in existence. But your life at this point is not just about surviving. The problem is that your attachment to surviving is what keeps you from truly living, from truly thriving. There is much more to life than maintaining that existence. Beginning today, you are going to put a permanent end to that absolutely false belief that your identity is you.

What you have just discovered is the key to setting yourself free for life. So take a few minutes and think about and process all of what has just come and is coming to you. Then jot some notes down about what you're getting.

_____

_____

_____

_____

_____

_____

_____

_____

_____

The Really Good News About Your Identity

1. Your identity is based on your perception of what happened, not what happened; therefore, it has nothing to do with the originating event. The real beauty behind that is if you experienced something tragic as a child and have blamed that event for why your life is the way it is, you can stop. From this moment on, your life can be whatever you want it to be. That means that you are now free to reframe your past and rewrite your future.

2. Your identity is literally millions and millions of steps away from the originating event. Each thought and emotion you have had all add up. Just think. If you have even 10,000 thoughts a day that are based in your survival decision (out of the 50,000 that you think daily), over a year, that's almost 4 million thoughts continually programming you.

3. When forming your identity (how you survive/get by in the world), you seek other's validation in the *Testing Stage*. But when your identity is formed, there is a complete reversal that instantly occurs. Once you know for sure that your identity is you, you will do whatever you can to never let anyone see "the real you" anymore. To illustrate, if you are a perfectionist, the reason you are that way is to cover up and to protect yourself from the judgments of others. You want to avoid their disapproval. The reason you want to avoid their disapproval is somewhere down deep inside, you are afraid that what they are saying matches the real you. Since you don't feel good about yourself, you don't

want anyone to validate those negative emotions so you do what you can to avoid anyone seeing them. If your emotions are extremely negative and you feel very bad about yourself, like you're an utter failure, you don't want any validation of that because if the world knows you're an utter failure, life is not very good at that point. In fact it may not even be worth living.

4. When you developed your identity, it wasn't your fault. You couldn't help the associations you made. Remember, you didn't have the reasoning ability or the capacity to think otherwise. The point is, you were just learning the rules of the game. You were just trying to learn how to survive. So you can stop blaming yourself right now. There is a tremendous freedom you instantly gain by doing that. To illustrate, I worked with a lady whose girlfriend's father molested her when she was five years old. When she told her parents, they punished her by not letting her see her friend anymore. She had a double whammy. Yet, none of it was her fault. For the next 37 years, she blamed herself by thinking she should have done something different. But she couldn't have. She did not invite his advances and she could not have stopped them any better than what she did. Yet she carried that guilt and pain all those years. The moment she realized it wasn't her fault, she was free.

5. Your identity is not you. So many people are afraid to let go of who they think they are for fear that there will be nothing left of them. Yet nothing could be farther from the truth. If you are not your fears, what's left is love. If you are not your doubts, worries and hang-ups, then what's left is the real you that has been held down for so long. That real you is a champion. That real you is magnificent. That real you is priceless. The only purpose of your identity is the same thing as your survival decision. It's just to keep your heart beating and nothing else. There is much more to life than just surviving. You can now go and thrive.

A Closing Thought About Beliefs

Once you understand your beliefs, how they formed and how they keep you stuck in habitual patterns and behaviors, you can begin immediately to be successful, happy, fulfilled and in love with life. Your identity forming beliefs were based in misconceptions, misunderstandings and misassociations. They have nothing to do with the pure magnificence and beauty that you truly are. They don't define you. Debbie Ford says in her book, <u>The Secret Of The Shadow,</u>

When we live in these stories, we engage in noisy internal dialogues, self-defeating habits and abusive behaviors. But once they are understood and processed, our traumas and failures, our pain and our discontent, will take us deep inside and return us to our Divine essence.

"You can succeed if others do not believe in you. But you cannot succeed if you don't believe in yourself." — Dr. Sydney Newton Bremer

Summary Of Key Ideas And Important Points

1. You must find your core, negative beliefs that "sponsor" all the rest of your thoughts.
2. Your identity has nothing to do with the original 'traumatic' event.
3. How you got to be who you are was not your fault. You were just learning to survive.
4. You can't change what you don't know.
5. Your beliefs create your reality whether you are aware of them or not.
6. You will never go for things you don't believe you can achieve.
7. You deserve the life of your dreams.
8. When you deal with a problem at its core, it doesn't come back anymore.
9. You have all the power to make your life anything you want to make it.
10. Your past does not equal your future.

CHAPTER 2

FORGIVE AND BE FREE

"Forgiveness is unconditional love in action."
– Darshan G. Shanti

This chapter is a deep look into the heart and soul of forgiveness. It will take you on a remarkable journey of warmth, grace and love. It will ask you to go to places you may not want to go, look at things you may not want to look at and it will ask you to do things you haven't wanted to do. It boldly asserts that to the degree that you forgive yourself and whomever or whatever you think has hurt you or offended you in some way, you will have a peace such that you have never known. What comes from that place of peace is sure to be miraculous. In fact, it is one of the greatest miracle makers in the world.

The benefits to forgiveness are tremendous. You'll have:

- Lower blood pressure
- Less stress
- Less anger
- Lower heart rate
- Lower risk of alcohol or substance abuse
- Reduced chances of depression
- Lower anxiety
- Reduction in chronic pain
- Greater energy
- Healthier friendships
- Greater religious or spiritual well-being
- Improved psychological well-being

To me, those are the minor benefits that happen by default. I promise you that the reward will be far more than you can ever imagine. It will literally change your life in unimaginably fantastic ways. And it could even save it.

On the other hand, holding onto resentments has the opposite effect of most of those. When you hold onto pain, old grudges, bitterness and even hatred, many areas of your life will be affected negatively. When you're unforgiving, you pay a very big price.

You'll experience more:

- Anger
- Confusion
- Sadness
- Sickness
- Bitterness
- Resentment
- Frustration
- Regret

And

- You'll get less accomplished
- You'll feel trapped
- You'll feel misunderstood more often

Clearly, those negatives are NOT WORTH IT. They suck the life out of you. They drain your energy and make you want to give up.

What Forgiveness Is And What It Does

According to Dr. Gerald Jampolsky, MD,

Forgiveness is the process of letting go of your negative judgments about other people and your negative judgments and self-condemnations about yourself.... Forgiveness is the willingness to give all of your anguish and anger up to a higher power and trust that it can be transformed into love.

I also say that forgiveness is unconditional love in action. It is a big key to your freedom, peace, ease and joy. Forgiveness is all about you. It is one of the greatest healing forces on the planet. Forgiveness is extremely powerful. It puts you in charge and in control of your life because it prevents you from being a victim. Forgiveness enables you to be responsible for your emotions. Forgiveness allows you to let go of resentments and anger. Forgiveness unties you from thoughts and feelings that bind you and it unites you with peace and harmony.

Next to I love you, I forgive you is probably the most powerful phrase that you can ever say. In the moment you mean those words, not just say them, you instantly feel better and the weight of the situation disappears. This is true no matter how long you've felt the way you've felt or how strong the feelings were. If you don't feel that way, then you haven't truly forgiven. There are no two ways about it.

Forgive And Forget...When Appropriate

Please understand that forgiving isn't the same as forgetting what happened to you. Although the past does not equal the future, you do learn by it. Many people advocate that you forgive and you forget. I believe that if you need to forgive yourself, you should do that and then forget it. Just leave it in your past where it belongs. I also believe that if someone did something to you that was extremely hurtful, you should forgive but you should also remember so as not to allow it to happen again. Whatever was done that hurt you may always remain a part of your life. But forgiveness helps you focus on what's important now. It helps you to W.I.N. (What's Important Now). What's important now is that you move on with your life. Forgiveness also doesn't mean that you deny the other people's responsibility in doing what they did, and it doesn't minimize or justify their actions. You can forgive the person without excusing the act. Mothers who forgive the people who killed their children do so to enable them to live their lives much more happily. And forgiveness brings them closure, relief and peace so they are free to move on.

An Extreme Need To Forgive

The tragic story of a two year old girl who died after her mother went to work and left her daughter in a locked car for eight hours as the temperature approached 100 degrees outside and came close to 150 degrees inside, illustrates profoundly the need to forgive. There are some people who believe this woman is guilty of horrible neglect and deserves to suffer greatly for what she did. Maybe that is so; maybe it is not. That's not for me to decide. Assuming she did accidentally forget about her sleeping baby, the inconsolable pain, the horrific agony that she must feel would be unimaginably unbearable. If she doesn't forgive herself, this will probably kill her. She will destroy herself with guilt and rage turned inward. She'll probably start drinking or taking pain killers to somehow numb herself. She may feel that she doesn't deserve anything good anymore. She may feel that she could never be happy anymore, let alone even deserving the right to be happy. She may see her future as completely bleak, hopeless and pointless. She may see nothing but pain and suffering for the rest of her life. My belief is that if she doesn't forgive herself, her life will be over.

She will always remember what happened and it will never, ever happen again. What forgiveness will enable her to do is to live the rest of her life productively, maybe dedicating it to child safety laws and becoming a lawyer who represents children who were abused by their parents. She would transform and possibly save many, many lives, including her own. Then her daughter's death would not have been in vain because it would have given her mother a purpose. Watch the film Erin Brockovich if you want to be inspired and see what one really dedicated woman can do if she really wants to. She is a champion. She is no different than you.

To Forgive Or Not To Forgive...
It's Always A Decision

Forgiveness is ALWAYS only a decision away. You can decide to forgive or not to forgive because you are the one who is in control of your thoughts and feelings and your beliefs and viewpoints. The fact that you think you need to forgive means that you believe something wrong was done to you. Maybe you had an expectation that was not met. Maybe someone made a promise and didn't keep it. Maybe it was worse than that and someone physically hurt you or a loved one. Whatever the case may be, when you don't forgive, it automatically puts you in a place where you are 'right' and they are 'wrong'. There is the choice and subsequently, the decision. Even if the entire world agrees with you that what happened was wrong, it doesn't matter. Forgiveness sets you free from that.

You may wonder how you can forgive those who you believe have really *wronged* or *hurt* you. You may wonder how it's possible to even consider it, let alone do it. You may question its effectiveness. You may not see the point in it. You may not want to forgive them or yourself. You may not think they (or you) deserve it. The very thought of it may aggravate you. That would be quite understandable. When hurt has been built up for so long, it becomes like water because it will always take the path of least resistance. And the water will keep wearing away the ground beneath it just as the hurt will keep wearing a pattern of thoughts, feelings and beliefs in your psyche. That path of hurt becomes tremendously difficult to escape from because it is so deep and so real.

By not forgiving ourselves for what we believe we should have done or what we should be doing vs. what we have done and are doing, we hold ourselves back in virtually every area. Somehow we believe that if we keep punishing ourselves over and over, then somehow we will be redeemed. We think that when we have paid a big enough price for long enough, then and only then do we deserve to be forgiven and/or to forgive ourselves.

Yet it's all hogwash. True forgiveness requires none of that. Read that again. True forgiveness requires none of that. True forgiveness is instantaneous the moment you decide you want to forgive. It comes as a result of a decision. You can decide at any time to forgive or not, but it's still your decision. Some say it's a process. Some say it takes time. But whether you decide for it to take ten years, ten minutes or ten seconds, it's still your decision how long you want to hold onto it.

Who Says Forgiveness Isn't Easy?

I can't tell you how many websites I visited and things I read while doing my research for this book that say it's hard to forgive. Look, we've all been *wronged*, *hurt*, *betrayed*, *used* and *treated poorly* at some point or another in our lives. We've all experienced life being unfair to us. Some of us have had far worse experiences than others. Some of us had parents who abused us physically, mentally, maybe sexually. People have stolen from us. People have lied to us. Our spouses and partners have cheated on us. The list of 'bad' things goes on and on. In other words, we've all had ample opportunities to forgive because we've all had many bad things that have happened to us.

We've also all had the chance at one point or another to play the victim role. People gladly give up their power in order to be right. They become victims to their circumstances or to others and use that as an excuse to be irresponsible and then they hold a grudge against those who they believe did them wrong.

I have watched countless people throw their lives away on drugs and alcohol because they weren't able to forgive themselves or their offenders. I have seen people sell out on themselves and their dreams and settle for a life that is little more than going through the motions. I have seen countless people beat themselves up day after day, week after week, month after month, year after year, decade after decade. I know this personally. I was one of them.

The Unforgivable Me

I believed somewhere, down very deep (below my conscious awareness) that I was unnecessary, that I was really nothing, a throw away, a waste and that no matter what I did, I was unforgivable. That is, I couldn't and wouldn't forgive myself and I couldn't and wouldn't let anyone else forgive me, not even God. As a result, my whole life was a struggle. It was a lie. It was a justification just to take up space. Keep in mind, I did not know what was causing me to operate this way. And it did not matter what personal growth work I did. Until I truly forgave myself, I stayed stuck.

It was hard for me to allow people to help me. I did not let people in. I did everything by myself. I was afraid to ask for anything because I feared the rejection. I feared being discovered and exposed. I feared the validation that I was really nothing and no good.

I was a walking excuse factory. I was a chameleon. I was a pretender. To the outside world, I was confident, competent, sure, powerful and full of compassion, grace, kindness and love. But inside, the exact opposite was true. I was in constant conflict, turmoil, perpetual upset and confusion. Nothing was working in my life even though I was doing all of the right things on the outside. I was a know-it-all. I closed my mind to a great deal of things because I would not let people contribute to me. It hurt my business in multiple ways. It cost me so much money I don't even want to think about it. I was extremely arrogant at times. I was rude. I was condescending. I was manipulative. It was amazing that anyone liked me. When they did, they didn't stay around for long. All of this came as a result of me not forgiving myself for who I believed myself to be.

Can you imagine how hard my life was? Can you imagine what my life satisfaction survey said? Life was no fun. It was full of pain and I experienced so little happiness that I often wondered what the point of it all was. In short, I was depressed, stressed and messed...up.

Forgiveness set me free from all of that virtually instantly. I finally forgave myself when I realized that I was doing all of that completely unconsciously to prove to myself and everyone around me that I was a good person. In other words, I made my whole life about everyone else to prove something that didn't need proving.

I have gone through hell and come out on the other side. Through the power of forgiveness, I now love myself and I allow myself to be loved. You may wonder if you can also do that. The answer to that is an indefatigable, YES! Because I have done it, I know you will be able to do it as well. Why do I know that? Because all I did was make a decision and I know that you're capable of making a decision to forgive yourself. Just begin now to think of yourself as the champion that you are. Know that you can do anything you set your mind to and anything you put your heart into. Believe you can. Trust yourself. Make a promise to yourself that whatever needs to be forgiven, you will indeed do.

The Do's And Don'ts Of Forgiveness

- You don't forgive because it's the right thing to do or that you think you'll look better or that you'll get something for it. You forgive because it is there to do.

- You forgive because it is in your highest and best good to do so.

- You forgive not from a logical place in your brain, but a feeling place in your heart, an energetic place if you would.

- You don't forgive out of a place of judgment. You forgive out of a place of openness.

- You don't forgive people because you think you are better than they are. That is righteous, arrogant and conceited. Being holier than thou is not forgiveness. It is a poorly disguised attempt to look good. In other words, forgiveness does not make you right and your offender wrong. That does nothing for you because you really haven't forgiven at all. When you forgive, you must be genuine and sincere.

- There are no levels of forgiveness. It's an all or nothing experience. If you only forgive part of what someone did, what good does that do?

- You don't have to like or accept the person in order to forgive him/her or what was done.

- You do have to want to forgive in order for it to be successful. If you do it begrudgingly, it won't work.

- Forgiveness is not about blame. Forgiveness is not about guilt. All is as it should be, for if it were not, it would be different.

"Forgiveness is the fragrance that the violet sheds on the heel that crushed it."
– Mark Twain

Forgiveness Begins With You

What you dislike about other people is really what you dislike about yourself. When you project your anger and hurt and other negative feelings onto others, you don't have to forgive yourself. There in lies the problem. When you make it about them, it's not your problem anymore. As Collin Tipping wrote in his beautiful book, <u>Radical Forgiveness,</u>

Metaphorically, we run a movie called Reality, through our mind (the projector), and we project it out there. Once we understand that what we call reality is just our projections, instead of blaming others we can begin to take responsibility for what we have created with our thoughts. When we change our perception and drop our attachment to our belief that what appears on the screen represents reality, we experience Radical Forgiveness.

Forgiveness is very self-centered. When you forgive someone else, it is not for them, it is for you. You instantly gain all of the benefits. But once again, let me caution you. **You don't forgive someone because you get the benefits. You get the benefits because you forgive**. When you come from an open and beautiful place in your heart, forgiveness doesn't need a reason. In that sense, all forgiveness is self-forgiveness. You can't forgive another without first forgiving yourself. And when you forgive yourself, the need to forgive others disappears.

The Reasons We Don't Forgive

- We get a lot of juice out of being right
- We don't believe we should have to because we did nothing wrong
- We believe forgiving is making what happened O.K.
- It makes us feel like we're in control and keeps us looking strong
- We don't really feel it inside ourselves
- We don't believe that 'they' deserve to be forgiven
- It keeps our survival decision firmly in place
- We don't believe any good would come of it
- We think forgiving them means forgetting what they did

There is a downside to all of those reasons. Being right only makes us right. It doesn't make us happy. When we live in our justifications and build up our cases against whoever wronged us, that keeps us stuck in a victim mentality. That keeps our survival decision solidly in place.

Now if you get nothing else out of this chapter, really take that last statement to heart. As we talked about in chapter one, we want to keep our survival decision intact at all costs. If we forgive someone, it may cause us to have to look at ourselves and the part we played in whatever happened.

To illustrate, if you look at a woman who has been abused physically and mentally for years, going from one bad relationship to the next, the point I am making will become clear. Each time she entered another relationship, she had an opportunity to forgive herself, to forgive her original *offender*, but by not doing it, she keeps her pattern in place. Remember, the insidious part is that she thinks she needs those negative beliefs because those beliefs form her identity and without that identity, she thinks she has nothing else. So, by not forgiving, she gets to keep the status quo. Everything is copasetic. All is as it should be in her world.

> "Sincere forgiveness isn't colored with expectations that the other person apologize or change. Don't worry whether or not they finally understand you. Love them and release them. Life feeds back truth to people in its own way and time—just like it does for you and me."
> – Sara Paddison

The Forgiveness
Practice

This process/tool/methodology is quite simple, although it may not be easy. You can use it to forgive anyone for anything at any time. You can use this process in any area of your life that bears forgiving. Take your time with each section. What's important is that you get to the core of it all, where the original hurt began. Do the work. Feel the feelings. Go through the process and don't skip over anything. Your freedom is at stake.

If you would like a full size template, go to www.the24hourchampion.com and click on the Templates tab, then click on 'The Forgiveness Practice'.

1. Write down the facts of what happened, minus all of the story and embellishments that typically go along with being upset, hurt or wronged.

_____

_____

_____

_____

2. Write down all of your thoughts about what happened. Get the entire story out. Write and write until you don't have anything left to say.

_____

_____

_____

_____

3. Write down exactly how you feel about what happened. Don't pull any punches. Feel all the anger, the hurt, the pain, the sadness, the rage. It's O.K. When you take a deep and honest look at yourself and how it really feels to maintain any negative feelings, you'll discover immediately that it's not worth it. So dig deep.

_____

_____

_____

_____

4. Usually there is a payoff (something positive you're getting) out of not forgiving. Take some time to think about what that might be and then write it down. The longer you think about this and the more you explore it, the more you will get much deeper levels of release. This step holds the key to your freedom.

_____

_____

_____

_____

5. Look for similar patterns in your life where this situation has occurred and write down what seems to be the common denominator between those events. In other words, was someone always taking advantage of you? Were you always the victim of something?

_____

_____

_____

_____

6. Look at the decisions you made about yourself and your world as a result. Did you decide you can't trust people? Did you decide that relationships are bad? Did you decide that you don't like yourself? Write down all negative decisions you've made. You may have to search for a while to find some of them. Just take your time and they will come to you.

_____

_____

_____

_____

7. Look closely at the results of all of those situations and write down your thoughts about why you would need to keep creating those results over and over again. For example, if you were abandoned as a child and as an adult, you keep picking relationships where your partner leaves, begin to examine why those results keep showing up.

_____

_____

_____

_____

8. Reframe the event and turn it into something positive. It may look horribly negative. And from one point of view, it may not appear to have any positive aspect to it, but keep looking. Look for the blessing in disguise in each situation. In other words, what did you learn about yourself and how can you use that to make your life better or the world better? People who have been the victim of gun crimes have gone onto become crusaders for gun control. People who have lost loved ones in hospitals due to malpractice have gone onto change the laws that save many lives.

_____

_____

_____

_____

9. List all of the positive benefits you'll get once you forgive what needs to be forgiven. When you find out how great those benefits are, you'll want to forgive yourself immediately.

_____

_____

_____

_____

10. Take whatever appropriate action is necessary. Write a letter. Make a phone call. Visit the person. Start a campaign or create a foundation if you feel compelled. Just jot some quick ideas down here. The last chapter will help you put a plan in place should you decide to do something big.

_____

_____

_____

_____

What you have just accomplished will have a purely miraculous effect in your life. I would love to hear them. Please feel free to email me and share your miracles.

A Forgiveness Letter

One of the best things you can do is to write a letter of forgiveness to yourself. Be brutally honest, real and truthful. You can't hide from yourself. Go deep. The purpose of the forgiveness letter is to get all the poison out of you. It's a cathartic process. It will free you, energize you and enable you to move on. Here is the actual letter that I wrote to myself many years ago. Use it as an example.

My Forgiveness Letter

I am writing this letter of forgiveness to me because I have poisoned myself for far too long and it hurts too much to continue living this way. And because I love myself and carrying all of my pain is incongruent with love, I can not and will not live that life anymore. I now forgive myself for all of the following things. I have withheld love from myself. I have berated myself, put myself down and knocked the shit out of myself. I have been so hard on me and I never gave myself any time to breathe. I spent most of my life in anger, in denial of my own bull shit, wallowing in my own self-righteous indignation. I have been a complete victim all the while swearing that I was OK and there was nothing that I wasn't doing to make my life better and so it wasn't my fault that my life wasn't working. Hell, it couldn't be. I was perfect. I blamed everyone else and I was right. I had the evidence. I never owned my greatness, my pricelessness, my magnificence because real deep down I didn't believe I was truly lovable. I didn't believe I could do anything that would make people love me and I wasn't good enough to be loved for who I was. So, I set myself up to never win. I was stuck because I wouldn't do the only thing I needed to do and that was to be myself. No, I could never be myself. I couldn't be myself because if I was, I thought I wouldn't be loved and I couldn't live without love. I have hurt myself by overeating and by eating poorly. I have abused my body. I have not exercised. I have not respected myself, valued myself, honored myself. I have not treated myself with dignity. I have sold out on myself, on my dreams, on my passions. I have given up too quickly. I have made too many excuses. I have in fact, been an excuse factory. I had an answer for everything. I've manipulated myself and others. I have never been responsible at the deepest levels of my being, but I sure acted like I was. I made people wrong and I've said hurtful things to the ones I love. I mistreated people and blamed them if they felt bad. After all, it wasn't my fault. I used my knowledge of human development to force them into changing. I did all this under the guise of helping people. Some help I was. I didn't listen to what people told me. I didn't listen to myself. I could not hear what was being told to me. I knew better. To admit it would have meant my very survival would have been in jeopardy. I have lied to myself, been untrue, unreal and not empathetic. In fact, I have been pathetic. I shut my feelings off. I worked on everyone else but me. I was fake. I was angry and I made people pay for my anger.

A Forgiveness Declaration

Once you go through the forgiveness practice and have written a forgiveness letter to yourself and to anyone you believe you need to forgive, you get to the point where forgiveness is almost not necessary. In other words, you've learned all that you can learn and gotten all the insights you needed to get. You come to the realization that forgiveness is a gift that you give yourself and it's for you primarily. If other people benefit, that's great, but that's not the purpose. If you need a little boost, just read this Declaration Of Forgiveness.

My Declaration Of Forgiveness

I, _____ now forgive _____ (insert the name or names) for doing/not doing, etc. _____ (insert the 'wrong') to me/my family/my friend, etc. I realize that by holding onto my resentment, I am only hurting myself and it does nothing to resolve the situation. What is done is done. The past has passed and there is nothing I can do about it now. All I can do now is move ahead with my life. I don't deserve to suffer. I don't need to punish myself or anyone else. I am responsible for how I feel and for what I do or don't do with my life. I owe it to myself to forgive. I realize that I played a part in the situation and I now see that what happened was a gift that enabled me to heal a part of myself that previously remained hidden and therefore kept me stuck. I now have a deep appreciation and am very grateful for the situation. I humbly, openly and freely forgive.

Make sure you put this declaration into your own words. When you are done reading it, check in with yourself regarding how you feel. If you still have any negative feelings, go back through the forgiveness practice. It simply means that there is something that you have not uncovered. Keep going through it until you feel (at the very least) neutral and preferably very good about the situation.

Now it's time to find out what's going on in your world. Take some time to really think about these questions. Feel their impact in your life and then make whatever decisions you need to make and start the forgiveness process.

Transformational Questions

1. **Who do you carry a grudge against or hold angry or resentful feelings toward and why? In other words, who haven't you forgiven? List all of the people that you can think of and jot a quick note down about why you hold that grudge next to each name you wrote.** Don't censor the list. You may have to look far back in your memory. You'll probably notice a pattern the further back you go. The grudge may just be with yourself. It could be with God. It could be with the Government, the IRS, your boss or anyone else.

_____

_____

_____

_____

2. **In what areas of your life have you not forgiven yourself?** You must be very honest here. Please don't hide behind a mask of false bravado. This is vital. The more areas you list, the more freedom you'll begin to experience.

_____

_____

_____

_____

3. Do you want to forgive yourself? Yes or No? _____ Why or why not?

_____

_____

4. **Do you want to forgive the people you believe to be the offenders? Yes or No?** _____ Why or why not?

_____

_____

_____

5. Is there anything holding you back from forgiving? In other words, what do you have to lose by forgiving? This is a very powerful question. If you have any negative associations with forgiveness, they will most surely surface here.

_____

_____

_____

6. What do you have to gain by forgiving yourself or others?

_____

_____

7. From the forgiveness practice, write the payoff you discovered.

_____

_____

_____

8. Is the payoff bringing you closer to what you want or taking you farther away from what you want? _____

9. If it's taking you farther away and costs you a great deal emotionally, does it make sense to keep doing it? Yes or No? _____

10. Describe how your life would be different if you could forgive those who have caused you pain. You have to want that life more than you want your resentments and judgments. That is, you have to want to live more than you want to survive. Forgiveness is all about freedom from all the resentments, blame, shame, guilt, hurt, pain, etc. that have held you back. As I like to say, "Forgiveness is unconditional love in action." The decision is completely up to you.

_____

_____

_____

_____

"You will know that forgiveness has begun
when you recall those who hurt you and feel
the power to wish them well."
— Lewis B. Smedes

Summary Of Key Ideas And Important Points

1. Forgiveness is always your decision.
2. Forgiveness can happen instantly.
3. Forgiveness has many blessings in disguise.
4. Forgiveness sets you free.
5. Forgiveness heals you and those around you.
6. Forgiveness is unconditional love in action.
7. Forgiveness is an amazing gift that you give yourself.
8. Forgiveness creates miracles.
9. Forgiveness is not forgetting; it's remembering without being encumbered.
10. Forgiveness enables you to move on with life and make a difference for others.

CHAPTER 3

TAKING TOTAL RESPONSIBILITY AND OWNERSHIP OF YOUR LIFE

"The price of greatness is responsibility." – Winston Churchill

This one chapter alone is literally the foundation of this book and the ultimately the rest of your life. Do whatever you have to do to ingrain the information into your head, heart, soul, mind and your conscious and unconscious.

Let me be as straightforward as possible regarding responsibility. The truth is that you are responsible for everything in your life. That means everything you do, think, feel, experience in your career, your relationships and every area of your life. Whether you want to be responsible or not, you are. There is no second option.

Perhaps more importantly, your life literally depends on it. What I mean by 'your life' is the life you really and truly want... the life of your dreams. If you are willing to be responsible, you can have that. If not, you'll have something less...much less.

The Random House Dictionary says that responsibility means, "Being the cause or reason for something."

Think about that for a moment. What are you the 'cause' of in your life or your business or your relationships or your health? In reality, you are the 'cause' of everything in your life...whether you want to be or not. That's the tough one for most people to swallow. But the sooner you arrive at accepting 100% responsibility for everything, the more successful you'll be. Ultimate power comes from accepting total responsibility. You want something more than you have now. Whether that is more success, more happiness, more fulfillment, more joy, more happiness, more money, more health, it really doesn't matter. The quickest key to begin to have all that you desire is responsibility.

As Dan Kennedy says in his book, <u>No B.S. Business Success The Ultimate No Holds Barred Kick Butt Take No Prisoners Tough And Spirited Guide</u>, "Go take a look in the mirror. There's the man or woman who can make you happy, thin, rich, famous, or whatever it is you aspire to. Dr. Phil can't make you thin. McDonald's doesn't make you fat."

The rock group "The Eagles" has their take as well. Here are some lyrics from the song, *Already Gone*. "I know it wasn't you who held me down. Heaven knows it wasn't you who set me free. So often times it happens that we live our lives in chains and we never know we even have the key."

Look, there are tons and tons of articles, books, reports and talks about responsibility, yet it astonishes me that even with all of those tools and resources available, irresponsibility runs so rampant. Just think of how many people you know who have given up. They settle for far less than they really could have. They become bored, resigning themselves to a life of mediocrity. Some of them drift through their lives aimlessly without purpose or passion. Is that you? If it is, it's time to do something about it.

People blame their parents, their circumstances, the economy, their friends, their teachers, etc., for their situation. They have more excuses and less happiness. They have *J*ustifications, *E*xcuses, *R*easons, *K*nowledge about why they can't have their life. If you look at the first letter of each of the italicized words, I am sure you'll see that they are being a *J.E.R.K.* The point is that you can be a *J.E.R.K.* or you can have your life, but you can't have both. A little later in this chapter, you'll do an exercise that will enable you to stop being a *J.E.R.K.*

Responsibility Sucks...
But It's The Only Thing That Works

My life partner, Ajanel said that to me one day and then she started teaching it to everyone. She learned that lesson after many unfortunate things happened to her and she had to be responsible for all of them even though none of the situations were caused by her. She thought it wasn't fair, but that didn't matter because what had to be done, had to be done. It puts responsibility in a whole new light. It's like we used to say in the military, "Suck it up and drive on."

One of my clients said to me, "I only want to be responsible for the good decisions I make. Let someone else be responsible for the bad ones." Of course that doesn't work. I have worked with many clients who are terribly unhappy and don't want to admit that they are responsible for their unhappiness. I ask them why they don't want to take responsibility. They tell me, "Because it's easier not to."

It does seem like it's much easier to place the blame on other people for what they did or didn't do to you or for you. But the truth is that while it may look so much easier, it is actually much harder. Being irresponsible causes stress, anxiety, pain, health problems, relationship problems and so much more. It's truly not worth it.

So why are people irresponsible when it costs them so much? Why are people irresponsible when there is so much pleasure, joy and fun to be experienced? I believe there are two things. First, it is taught and taught and taught to us from an early age by the models we see on TV and virtually everywhere else. And, I believe it is the negative associations people have with being responsible.

My clients have told me that to be responsible means they are going to experience pain, be controlled, be hurt, have no freedom, that it will cause them anger and frustration. That may be true if things have been out of balance for a long time. And it may take a great deal of work to get their life back in order. Depending on what it is that they have been avoiding, they may have to eat a whole bunch of humble pie. And, there may be some pain or a lot of pain involved in the beginning. In fact, becoming responsible often involves getting past some initial discomfort, some pain and some fear. However, when you're on the other side of it, you'll be much happier.

The point is there are consequences to everything we do or don't do. If the consequences in your life now are severe because you have been avoiding responsibility in a certain area for a long time, that should give you a great deal of incentive to never let that happen again.

When you can take responsibility for yourself fully, you are free and it's empowering to the nth degree. That means all the 'good' and all the 'bad' stuff. Notice I did not say 'some' of the bad and 'all' of the good. Being responsible is an all or nothing game. Winner take all, as it were. When I share that with people, they seem to be shocked and almost in disbelief. To them it is a radically new concept and one that they've never considered.

If you've been avoiding being fully responsible, I would offer you this. Focus on all of the great things that will happen to you, not the negative or painful things you think you'll have to go through. It's really never as bad as people imagine it to be, but it sure is a whole lot more pleasurable.

The Greatest Responsibility Of All

For the purpose of this chapter about responsibility, though, I am taking direct aim on one specific area. It is the responsibility to put yourself first, your dreams first, your happiness first, your needs first. I am talking about you putting yourself at the top of your list. I am talking about never leaving yourself out of your life's equation ever again. I am talking about you being your number one priority.

Now that might fly in the face of what you have been taught and that's O.K. Most of us have been taught to always think of others and put their needs first. Yet I'm here to tell you that putting other's wants and needs before your own (all the time) is one of the causes for great unhappiness and dissatisfaction. On the other hand, putting yourself first makes a great deal of sense when you think about it. You can't take care of anyone else until you can take care of yourself. I learned that in one of my first jobs.

Years and years ago, I was an emergency medical technician. One of the first things we were taught when we came upon an accident scene was to do a site survey. We were told to make sure we carefully looked all around the accident scene first. Why? Because if there was an electrical wire dangling and we got electrocuted, then not only could we not help the people we came to help, but we made the situation worse because now there were more casualties.

Here's another example. Think of the last time you flew. The flight attendants tell you that if you're traveling with a small child and the oxygen masks drop down, you need to put the mask on yourself first and then the child. Once again, if you put the mask on the child first and you pass out, who is going to take care of the child?

You May Need To Thicken Your Skin

Let me forewarn you. If you start putting yourself and your needs first, there are some people that won't like it. In fact, some will resent it quite heavily. They will come right out and tell you. They'll put you down. They may make you wrong. They may attack you and call you selfish. Actually, you are not being selfish at all. You are being self-centered. And that's a very good thing. I'll explain the difference between being selfish and self-centered as I have come to understand it. Selfishness is rooted in survival. It is fear based. It's like a two-year old having a temper tantrum because you take his toy away from him. Selfish people want everything for themselves and they don't want to share. They don't care how anyone feels because they are only concerned with themselves, their wants and their needs.

Self-centered people are polar opposites. They have a very healthy regard and respect for themselves and others. Their self-esteem is very high. They are confident and competent. They know that there's enough to go around so they take care of themselves first and then they are able to take care of others.

I learned a long time ago that I live my life for me. When I didn't and I constantly made everyone and everything more important than me, it almost killed me. Yes, you read that right. It almost killed me. I'll explain.

I Almost Paid The Ultimate Price

I have been in the personal development business for eight years full time. I have been studying it for two decades. During that time, I have put over 40,000 hours of work in. I have worked with over 30,000 people from students to people in their 80's. I gave my heart and my soul to everyone I ever worked with and I paid the price with my health.

My story starts over ten years ago. I was a bright eyed, go-getter on a mission to make a difference in the world. Like many entrepreneurs, I was working eighteen-hour days, just trying to stay afloat. But the stress, anxiety and lack of sleep that typically come with the entrepreneurial lifestyle quickly began taking their toll on me.

It started with acid reflux. You know, that burning in the pit of your belly that quickly makes its way up your chest. It causes terrible pain that just won't quit. When I did find some time to sleep, it wasn't very restful. The stress of looming bills, making the next sale, the constant worry and anxiety over what was going to happen and the burning pain in my chest were just partly to blame.

But like many entrepreneurs, I ignored the warning signs and pushed on. My family and friends told me that I needed a vacation. They begged me to slow down and relax. Instead I worked even longer hours just to keep my head above water. I was sure living the American dream! Yeah right. As if things weren't bad enough, the stress and anxiety got so bad that I developed sleep apnea. If you don't know what this is, consider yourself lucky. Sleep apnea is when you stop breathing while you are asleep (in my case about once per minute) and are then jarred awake by your oxygen starved body reminding you to start breathing again. My case was so bad that I would wake up more than 60 times an hour. That means that once a minute I was waking up and as a result, I never entered deep sleep. I was sleeping a total of less than one-hour per night…if even that! I was confused. My memory was terrible. I couldn't think clearly. I became very angry and intolerant. In short, I was a mess! I still ignored the warning signs and kept pushing forward.

Things got really bad when I received the crashing blow…my doctor told me that I had multiple sclerosis. That is a disease in which my own body was eating away at me. I was basically killing myself just to survive (if you could even call what I was doing, surviving). I looked terrible. I felt terrible and my relationships were strained almost beyond repair. My life was unraveling at the seams right before my eyes. I even began to fill out the mountain of paperwork necessary to collect social security disability because I was no longer able to function on any kind of productive level. Although I was never one to give up…I started to tie up my loose ends and prepare for what I thought was inevitable. Yes, I thought I was going to die. At that point, there didn't seem to be any hope. I remember thinking to myself while I was having lunch with Jim Campbell, the person who wrote the foreword, "Am I ever going to see him again?" and "What is he going to say at my funeral?"

For me, feeling hopeless and helpless is probably the worst feeling on the planet, but I had reached the end of all my ropes and did not know where to turn. What happened next was purely a miracle…divine intervention, if you will.

A few weeks later I was having a conversation with someone and I said, "All these problems I am having are probably due to the fact that I am not being responsible about something." She agreed. But what was it? I knew that if I didn't discover the root cause and take total responsibility for it, that I was not going to be around on the planet much more.

So I immediately went to work on myself. I probed deep into my unconscious and systematically began taking my life apart. I worked on myself for months. The more I dug, the more I discovered and the better I began to feel. Layer after layer of problems and challenges melted off of me. I felt stronger and more alive with each passing day.

To make a long story short, it turned out that many of the problems I was experiencing were not caused by nutritional deficiencies, germs, or the other likely culprits…they were caused by the self-imposed stress and anxiety that I was creating due to my refusal to take full responsibility for my life.

Once I took myself out of that situation, my life turned around almost over night. In fact, I was told (by the same medical doctors) who had been treating me as an MS patient that I no longer had the disease. In addition, my sleep apnea is gone and I do not consume one little purple pill for acid reflux anymore because it is also a thing of the past. My relationships have all improved. I am more successful than ever. My business is thriving. I work less and achieve much more than ever. In short, every single area of my life is much, much better.

I don't tell you that story to impress you, but rather to impress upon you that being irresponsible to myself and putting everyone else first almost killed me.

If you don't want to go down that path, or if you're already there and want to get out, I suggest you read this next statement very carefully. In fact, I suggest you commit it to memory. I suggest you post it in several rooms of your house and even in your car where you have no choice but to see it. Go to www.the24hourchampion.com and click on the Templates tab and click on 'Responsibility Quote' and get your own copy for FREE. It's already set up so it fits beautifully on an 8.5x11 page.

"The Moment I Take Full Responsibility For:
My Greatness
My Magnificence
My Pricelessness
And Love Myself Unconditionally
Then Live That Way <u>Without Exception</u>,
That's When I'll End All Of My Internal Struggle And Once And For All,
Have The Life I Have Always Wanted!"

When you read that, what does it communicate to you? What meaning do you take from it? How does it make you feel? Don't just say it makes logical sense and keep reading. Really take it to heart. Be with it. Read it over and over and over until it bypasses the normal obstacles your ego throws up. You see, if you read it once, it may occur like a good idea, but it won't be internalized. Your goal is to internalize it on every level you can. It doesn't matter if you have to read it one thousand times or more (not necessarily right now). It needs to sink in and get into your unconscious where it can take root. If you say to yourself, "That's ridiculous. I'm not going to read it 1000 times," it's just your unconscious beliefs dictating your success. You don't have to listen to it and you shouldn't. Think of it this way. If just reading that 1000 times gave you the life of your dreams, wouldn't it be worth it? That's where you have to put your focus. Don't focus on what a pain it would be to read it that many times. Don't doubt it. Don't assume it can't work. Remember, your thoughts create your reality.

The Pinky Exercise

This exercise will immediately help you to internalize the responsibility quote. Follow along and do exactly as I suggest. I am going to be telling you to do some weird sounding things. Just act as if I could do everything I am about to tell you, even though I can't.

Take a look at the pinky of your right hand. Think about its value. If I was to offer you a million dollars for just the top of it, would you take it? I promise you won't feel a thing. It won't get infected and it will heal instantly but it won't grow back. It will just look like you never had the top of your pinky. You won't get arthritis. Plain and simple, you'll have no problems with your pinky from now until the day you die.

Now, please don't think about what you could spend the money on. It's just a value for value exchange. For example, if I said I would give you a million dollars for the socks you're wearing, you wouldn't even hesitate. It's the same for your pinky. Is the top of your pinky worth one million dollars?

If you say it is worth more, I'll tell you what, you can have one billion dollars for it. Would you sell it for that much? If your answer is yes, then we'll move on to your entire pinky. Is that for sale? If so, how much? Whatever price you come up with doesn't really matter. I will buy all of your fingers for as much money as you want if you keep selling them. Eventually you're going to get to the point where you don't want to sell anymore. For some of you, that might be immediately because you won't even sell the top of your pinky. For others, you might sell your pinky and stop. For some, you'll sell another finger or two. I've done this with people who have sold me both of their arms for a measly twenty-million dollars.

So what's the point I am making with this exercise? The point is that if just a pinky or a few fingers are worth whatever price you came up with, then what is the rest of you worth? There is only one answer to that. It is priceless. In other words, you have so much value that you can't put a price on it. You are an im-measurable treasure. From now on, you can look at your pinky if you're going through a tough time and say, "I'm priceless. I'll get through this." When you really get that you're priceless, everything else will change in your life. Priceless people don't abuse their bodies with alcohol, drugs, food, nicotine. Priceless people love, value, honor, respect and cherish themselves. Priceless people are champions. You are priceless; therefore, you are a champion. The moment you truly realize that, no matter how bad your situation may be, you can begin to turn it around.

The question is, do you treat yourself like you are worth that much? If you don't, just realize this: You are either priceless or you are worth less. There is a space between worth and less because you are not worthless but you may believe you are worth less. Either one is your decision. Whether you understand it yet or not, you are priceless. You can't be any other way. If you don't believe that or start to argue with it by listing your faults, why would you do that? Why would you argue for your limitations? Why would you argue for your negative beliefs about yourself? The truth is, the real conscious you wouldn't. But when you start to argue for your smallness, it means that your unconscious is in control and so it gets its way.

The problems that most people have in their lives, relationships, careers, etc. are directly related to them not taking 100% responsibility for their great-ness, magnificence, pricelessness and not loving themselves unconditionally. When people don't do those things, they sell-out on themselves. They settle. They don't take risks. They justify their lives away. They are less happy, less fulfilled, less satisfied. It causes them to have a fear of failure, a fear of success, a fear of rejection.

As Henry David Thoreau pointed out, "Most men lead lives of quiet desperation and go to the grave with the song still in them." That's because they believe they are worth less. They believe they are not good enough. And they keep believing that all of their lives. It becomes their reality because it is their identity. When my clients tell me that they're not good enough, I ask them to tell me what they are comparing themselves to. Their belief that they don't measure up is so deeply ingrained that it never occurs to them that it might not be true. In their minds they are just not good enough and that's all there is to it. Well, I'm here to tell you that you do measure up. In fact, you can not, not measure up. Begin right now to take responsibility and believe in the truth. You are priceless. Focus on that. Breathe it in. Meditate on it. Accept it. Allow it to take you over for just a few minutes. Feel the good feelings it brings you. Bask in them. Soak them in. You'll never want to feel the feelings that being irresponsible brings ever again. And you won't be like so many great and talented people who you will never know the life of a champion because they didn't want to be responsible.

Just think of the artists who are too afraid to put their work out in the real world or the salespeople who don't sell very much because they are too afraid to ask for the business. Think of all of the famous people whose lives are complete train wrecks or who have committed suicide. Do you think those people value, love, appreciate, respect or honor themselves? Of course they don't. They feel terrible about who they are on some very deep level. They are terrified that the world will see the real them and so their public lives are just a mask to protect themselves from anyone 'seeing' who they are. If they loved themselves unconditionally, would they have those fears, doubts, insecurities? No they wouldn't because the context of their lives would be based in love and not in fear. So too it is for you.

The rest of this chapter will be devoted to helping you to realize (make real) that your life absolutely, positively needs to be based in love and being 100% responsible is how you achieve that.

So let's start by asking some questions about responsibility. To begin with, you need to define it for yourself. Most people I have worked with have only a vague idea of what responsibility means to them. Many of them don't want to define it because then they will have to admit they are not living that way.

Transformational Questions

1. What does taking total responsibility for your life and everything that you do, think, feel, experience, etc., mean to you? Don't write the results of being responsible. Just write your own definition.

_____

_____

_____

_____

2. Do you really live your life based on what you just wrote? Yes or No? _____

3. If not, why not?

_____

_____

So what were your answers? Once again, if you didn't answer them, you are being irresponsible to yourself. Go back and answer them now. Then go on. Everything builds on the previous section.

Take a look at your answer to question three. Whatever you wrote there (or didn't write, but thought about) are the excuses you give as to why you are not responsible. If you have written several reasons, you have a decision to make. If you don't make that decision, nothing is going to change in your life. That will also help you to answer the question properly. You're going to have to be really honest. You may not want to because it may be hard to look at. It may be quite painful. Look anyway.

4. What negative associations do you have with responsibility?

_____

_____

_____

_____

5. **What are all the areas of your life that you are not being totally responsible about right now?** Here is a tricky one. For years I took personal development seminars knowing that I was not going to deal with the one thing that I needed to deal with (my deep self-loathing). Consequently, my life was just a rehash of my past. So make sure you write down all of the areas you are not being responsible about, not just the surface level ones.

_____

_____

_____

_____

Once you get them down on paper, you can start to do something about them. But until you decide to be honest and take full responsibility (even for the areas in your life that you don't want to) nothing will change for the better. Please honor yourself and put that 'one thing' down that you've been avoiding forever. Yes it will be painful, but the relief on the other side will be beyond words. I promise you, you'll be OK.

Now go onto question six. Dig deep here. Don't just write surface level stuff. For example, if one of your excuses is that you're lazy, that's not enough. Even if you say to yourself, "But it's true, I am lazy," take it deeper. When people are lazy, it's because they are avoiding some kind of pain and the pain they are avoiding is usually related to some kind of fear which is ultimately rooted in some kind of negative belief they have about themselves.

6. What excuses have you given about why you haven't done those things you listed in question five?_____

_____

_____

_____

Let's take a small break from these questions so I can introduce you to a fundamental motivator behind all human behavior.

The Pain/Pleasure Principle

As humans, we are all motivated by avoiding pain or by gaining pleasure. People will do almost anything to avoid doing the things they find painful... even if it's something they say they want to do.

Take quitting smoking for example. People say they want to quit but they believe it will be far too painful to go through the withdrawals, so they avoid the pain of quitting. Until it becomes more painful for them to keep smoking, they will continue. Some people never even get there. How many people do you know who continue to smoke even when diagnosed with a deadly disease? For example, John Smith smokes and has cancer. The doctor's tell him that he must quit to have any chance at saving his life. His ego reasons that, "As bad as it is now, it would be far worse if John had to go through the pain of withdrawals," so it starts justifying why he can't quit. It says, "It would be too stressful and that would make his cancer worse." And that's the never-ending game it plays.

The avoidance of pain and/or the gaining of pleasure go into virtually every decision we make. We do or don't do things because of the pain it will bring us or the pain we will avoid and for the pleasure we will get (or not).

Here's where most people get stuck. They are afraid to change. They are afraid of the unknown. They are afraid of losing what they already have. All that fear represents pain. So, there is more pleasure for them to stay where they are. As a result, they don't take any action. They stay right where they are or they run the other way.

Now, if it is incredibly painful to stay in the situation you're in, but it's still more painful to change, you won't do it. It's the old, 'damned if I do and damned if I don't' scenario. In other words, when the pain of being irresponsible far outweighs the pain of being responsible, you will change. The good news is that you're the one who is in control of the whole thing. You get to say what is painful and what is not. You get to say how much pain you're willing to put up with or not.

I'll demonstrate that with this illustration. Take a look around you and pick any object that is about ten feet in front of you. That object is going to represent a very important goal or dream that you have. Now if nothing was blocking you from reaching that goal, you would walk right to it, grab it and that would be that. You would have easily reached it. However, in life it doesn't usually work that way. It's never that easy. In fact, there's always some sort of pain involved with achieving your dreams. So, to represent the pain that you might experience in going for your dream, imagine that lying in front of you is one-thousand rusty nails and thousands of shards of broken glass, a few black widow spiders, some pit vipers and some scorpions. In order to attain your goal, you must walk barefoot over and through all of that. What are you most likely to do? That's right. You're going to avoid it like the plague. You're not even going to walk around the nails and glass. Instead, you're going to look at your dream and start to diminish it. You're going to start to find all kinds of reasons why you don't really want it, why it's really not that important. In other words, instead of walking over the glass (going through the pain to reach your dreams) you'll reason that your dreams aren't worth it. Now, when the pain of staying where you are, far outweighs the pain of change, you'll move rapidly. Here's how you do that. You simply create more pain to not have what you want. So if you knew you would be killed by one of the snakes if you stood there, that would be far too painful and no doubt, you would start taking some giant leaps to your goal because the pain of dying far outweighs the pain of running over those nails.

Although that example is never going to happen, it does work as a metaphor for your life. You make excuses to avoid living the life you've always wanted because for some reason it is too painful to have that life. In my own case, for years I put off writing a book because it is a lot of work, because it takes a great deal of time, because it wouldn't be the best use of my time, etc., etc. The point was that it was far too painful for me to write the book...so I didn't.

So what changed? Why did I decide to write it? How did I decide to get myself to take action? I simply created a ton of pain to not write it. In other words, it became too painful for me not to write it. How I did that was I projected my current beliefs into the future and I didn't like what I saw. In fact, it disgusted me. I saw myself as a failure, broke emotionally, mentally and monetarily, wandering around saying to myself, "I wish I would have written that book." It was then that I was able to reverse my pain/pleasure principle. In that moment I was free to write the book.

Reversing Your Pain/Pleasure Principle

The following exercise is going to help you create all the pain (motivation) you'll need to help you to move rapidly ahead. What you need to do is to create as much pain in this exercise as you can. It will be like that snake that was going to bite you if you continued to stay where you were. You're going to look into your own future and imagine what your life will be like one, five, ten and twenty years from now if you keep on living as if all of your Justifications, Excuses, Reasons and Knowledge. (J.E.R.K.) are true.

Answer the following questions to begin right now to reverse your pain/pleasure principle.

At this very moment, how do I feel about myself? If you've sold out on yourself and your dreams and you've made tons of excuses, how does that feel? I am only looking for the negatives that you feel. Just go there. Some of my clients have said that they are disgusted with themselves and they feel horrible, like their life has been a waste. When you write how you feel, think along those lines. In spite of me sharing that, some of you are going to want to put positive things down because of all the growing you've done and all your new a-has. If you do, this exercise won't work.

_____

_____

_____

_____

Now, project those same thoughts and feelings out _1 year from now_ and describe what my life looks like in terms of my:

Relationships with my family/partner _____

_____

_____

Relationships with my friends _____

_____

_____

Relationship with myself. In other words, how do I now feel about myself?

_____

_____

_____

Money

_____

_____

Career _____

_____

_____

Now, project those same thoughts and feelings out _5 years from now_ and describe what my life looks like in terms of my:

Relationships with my family/partner _____

_____

_____

Relationships with my friends _____

_____

_____

Relationship with myself. In other words, how do I now feel about myself?

_____

_____

_____

Money

_____

_____

Career _____

_____

_____

Now, project those same thoughts and feelings out _10 years from now_ and describe what my life looks like in terms of my:

Relationships with my family/partner _____

_____

_____

Relationships with my friends _____

_____

_____

_____

Relationship with myself. In other words, how do I now feel about myself?

_____

_____

_____

Money _____

_____

_____

Career _____

_____

Now, project those same thoughts and feelings out _20 years from now_ and describe what my life looks like in terms of my:

Relationships with my family/partner _____

_____

_____

Relationships with my friends _____

_____

_____

Relationship with myself. In other words, how do I now feel about myself?

_____

_____

_____

Money _____

_____

Career _____

_____

_____

How was that? What did you learn about yourself? Twenty years from now, life probably looks really bad. I have had many people not even be able to get past five years. They simply said that knowing what they know now, if they continued doing what they've been doing, life wouldn't be worth living. They got the point. If you look at the costs you just wrote and say to yourself, "They're no big deal." It just means you haven't created enough pain yet. That's because your ego was doing its job.

The Ego's Job

Your ego's job is to protect you from pain. It doesn't want you to get hurt. It puts a protective bubble around you called, *The Comfort Zone*. It wants to do whatever it can to keep you comfortable. Your ego is faithful to the end. It's on constant vigil looking out for your own best interest. It does its job 24/7 and never whines, moans or complains. It's like a big watch dog that keeps anything away from you that IT considers to be a possible threat. It may not be a threat in reality, but from the ego's perspective, if it thinks that your survival is at risk, it will do whatever it can to make you avoid it. Take public speaking for example. It is the number one fear. Studies show that people had a greater fear of public speaking than they did of being killed in a fire. The fire is the real threat. So why would people be more afraid to public speak? Well, it goes back once again to your unconscious beliefs. People don't want their core, negative beliefs discovered. They think that if they are on stage that people will see who they really are. They believe that who they really are is worth less, not good enough, wrong, etc. As a result, they do whatever they can to avoid anyone finding out their hidden truth.

So the moment you start feeling pain, the ego comes up with all kinds of smoke screens, justifications, rationalizations and whatever else it has to do so that you won't go there. Even if your life is tremendously painful now, if your ego thinks that you will have worse pain if you do something new, it will do what it can to stop you. The ultimate pain is non-existence and the ego's job is to make sure that you survive at all costs.

The problem is your ego hasn't been trained. It thinks that it has carte blanche to do whatever it wants, however it wants to protect you. But like a dog, it has to be trained. It has to be told what to do. You have to set boundaries for it. Metaphorically speaking, you have to be the pack leader. When you do that, your ego will be your best friend and you two will work very well together.

Your ego won't be putting up defenses anymore. Excuses will start to fade away. You will start being more and more responsible. Life will become much easier. How you set boundaries for your ego is quite simple. All you have to do is change what you associate pain and pleasure to. You do that by asking a question. In other words, if taking a risk is painful and as a result you never do it, simply ask yourself what will it cost you (what will the pain be) if you don't take the risk? So instead of thinking that taking a risk is painful and NOT taking a risk is pleasureful, when you reverse the pain/pleasure principle, NOT taking a risk will be painful and taking the risk will be pleasureful.

The point is that when you are conscious, you have the power at all times. Your ego is under your control. Your wish is its command...NOT the other way around.

So if the costs that you just wrote in the pain worksheets are big enough, then you can immediately reverse your pain/pleasure principle. And your answer to question seven should be a big, NO. Once again, if it is not, simply go deeper into the costs and create more pain to stay where you are.

7. **Are you willing to continue to pay those prices?** Yes or No? _____

The key to question eight is action. In fact, you have to start being responsible in order to do things differently than you did before. You could easily write a bunch of stuff here and decide not to stick to it. If you find yourself making excuses about why you're not sticking to your plan, then simply create more pain or create more pleasure. When you're finished with question eight, you'll have the beginnings of a plan. Stick to that plan and your life will begin to turn around very quickly.

8. **If your answer is NO, who are you going to be and what are you going to do differently now to make sure that you don't keep paying those costs?** _____

_____

_____

_____

For question nine, when you first get started building your responsibility muscle, you may often need help from someone else to help hold you accountable. You need to pick someone who you know will hold your feet to the fire. Pick someone who is not afraid of a little friction. Don't pick someone who is going to let you slip and slide all around your agreements. You can do that on your own. Also, you need to set a definite time by when you are going to find your partner. Next week is not good enough. Be specific. Realistically, it should be today or tomorrow at the latest.

9. **Will you make an agreement with yourself and someone who will help hold you accountable to your promises?** Yes or No? _____ By when? _____ Who? _____

What will help you to do that is to keep your word. If you don't keep your word, everything you will have done so far will have been in vain. This is vital to your success. Think about it carefully. Answer question ten.

10. **In order to keep those agreements you made, you will need to keep your word. Will you?** Yes or No? _____ What does keeping your word mean to you? _____

At this point, your heart may be racing with anticipation? You may be afraid? You may be feeling tense. You may feel anxious. If so, it's perfectly all right. Don't worry. Your fears will soon subside and change into excitement as you begin at once to take full responsibility for your life. As Helen Keller says, "It's OK to have butterflies in your stomach. Just get them to fly in formation."

Choices And Decisions

I am going to share a very important distinction with you that you will use throughout this book and for the rest of your life. You're going to learn the difference between choices and decisions and discover how powerful decisions are. My guess is that you've never considered choices and decisions as anything special. Well if that's the case, it's all going to change from this moment on. To begin with, you need to understand what a choice is as opposed to a decision.

What Is A Choice?

Choices are options to pick from. In fact, there are 1000's of different types of foods you could choose from and there are millions of different movies, articles of clothing, activities, etc. to choose from. Out of all those choices (options to pick from) you make a decision. In other words, you first have the choice (options to pick from), and then you do something with the choice. That something is a decision. People refer to choices as something they make. In reality, they are referring to decisions. The only way you can "make a choice" is to "create an option" that did not exist before. Make sure you get that clear before reading on. Once again, choices are just options.

For this example, we will use a choice of cherry pie or broccoli.

What Is A Decision?

Take a look at the following words. What do they all have in common?

Sui<u>cide</u>, Pesti<u>cide</u>, Homi<u>cide</u>, Geno<u>cide</u>, De<u>cide</u>

They all end in the suffix *cide*. Cide means to kill or to cut off. Suicide means to kill self. Pesticide means to kill bugs. Homicide means to kill another person. Genocide means to kill a race of people. Then there is, decide. What it means is to kill a choice or an option. So once again, when you decide to do something, you look at all the options (choices) and then you pick one. You make the decision depending on which side has more pros or cons or which side has the stronger pros or cons. So if you're hungry right now and you want some quick energy and a taste that is sensational, you'll go for the cherry pie. If you were just diagnosed with diabetes and you're hungry and you want something sensational, you'll go for the broccoli because all the pros of eating cherry pie don't outweigh the one con of possibly getting very ill from all the sugar.

Really, pros and cons are just pain and pleasure said a different way. We always make decisions to bring us some kind of pleasure or help us to avoid some kind of pain. That is just how we are wired as human beings.

Cherry Pie
PROS/CONS
+ -
+ -
+ -
+ -
+ -
Pleasure/Pain

Broccoli
PROS/CONS
+ -
+ -
+ -
+ -
+ -
Pleasure/Pain

The Power And Freedom of Decision

There is a tremendous amount of power and freedom when you take full responsibility for all of your decisions. When I share that with people, it seems to go in one ear and out the other. They don't really hear it because they don't want to hear it. The point is, your decisions are yours and yours alone. That means that you can't blame anyone or anything else for how your life works or doesn't as a result of the decisions you make.

Read the following list of thirty decisions. Put a star next to any of them that really apply to you now or at any point in your life.

1. I decide to be happy or not.
2. I decide to be sad or not.
3. I decide to be angry or not.
4. I decide to attack in anger or not.
5. I decide to forgive or not.
6. I decide to seek revenge or not.
7. I decide to hold grudges or not.
8. I decide to stay where I am or not.
9. I decide to take action and move on.
10. I decide how long I want to feel any emotion or not.
11. I decide to eat poorly or not.
12. I decide to exercise or not.

13. I decide to smoke or not.
14. I decide to quit or not.
15. I decide how hard it will be to break any addiction or not.
16. I decide how easy it will be to break any addiction or not.
17. I decide to love or not.
18. I decide to allow myself to be loved or not.
19. I decide whom I want in my life or not.
20. I decide to be a success or not.
21. I decide to be a failure or not.
22. I decide to have abundance or not.
23. I decide I don't have enough or not.
24. I decide to be afraid to take risks or not.
25. I decide to be confident or not.
26. I decide to keep my word or not.
27. I decide to do what I say I will do or not.
28. I decide how my life works or not.
29. I decide to be irresponsible or not.
30. I decide to be priceless or not.

Do you believe ALL of those things? Do you really believe that you are completely responsible for all of your decisions? If you believe that anything outside of you is responsible for the things you do, you're a victim. If you ever find yourself complaining about the way things are, other people, your job, your family, your lack of money, happiness, joy, satisfaction, etc., take a look at what decisions you've been making. The point is, if you find yourself complaining, ask yourself, "Why would I be complaining about the decisions I make?"

Usually it is because if you complain about your situation, you don't have to do anything about it. You don't have to be responsible. Being responsible or not being responsible is a decision.

There is a very big pitfall to watch out for. You can become responsible about being irresponsible. But, that still makes you irresponsible. If you say things like, "I know I'm overeating, but..." I know I am smoking, but... "I know I am not keeping my word, but..." That's like saying, "I know I am being irresponsible now, but..." When you do that, you are manipulating yourself. You are a victim. And that leaves you powerless. Knowing you're being irresponsible does not absolve you from being responsible. Once again, you are responsible for everything in your life whether you want to be or not, whether you acknowledge that or not and whether you are conscious of it or not.

Now what you need to understand is that whatever decisions you make (good or bad) are your decisions. This is where taking 100% responsibility comes in. If you are not where you want to be in your life, it's your decision. It's your decision to take whatever action you must take to get you out of the place you're in. It's your decision not to take action as well. It's your decision to blame your circumstances, the economy, your boss, your family. It's also your decision to not blame any of them. When you make a decision, it's yours.

The following exercise will enable you to make one of the most powerful decisions you can make in your life.

The Triangle And The Circle

This simple concept that I am about to share with you will help you to really understand the decision you have in front of you. That decision is to accept full responsibility for your pricelessness or continue living the way you are now. This exercise is so simple and yet it is so profound that it will have a tremendous effect on the way you view yourself and your future. Even better than that, once you understand it, you'll be able to use it at any time to instantly change how you feel about yourself and you'll be able to use this tool to create a brand new future. So, I am going to ask you a question that may sound strange. Just go with it and you'll see how it works its way out.

If you're a triangle and you want to be a circle, how do you be a circle?

Now stay with me here. This exercise may sound silly and you may start to wonder what this has to do with your life, but I assure you that once you understand it, the impact will be quite deep.

At this point, most people look at that and say, "I'll just expand my sides and round off my corners and then I'll be a circle." But all that does is make the triangle look funny. In effect, it is a triangle "trying" to be a circle, but it is not a circle.

So, once again, if you're a triangle and you want to be a circle, how do you be a circle? Think about this. Take some time. Stop reading. Keep thinking. Can you be a circle if you're a triangle? The answer to that is NO! Then that begs the question. How do you be a circle if you're a triangle? If you're thoroughly confused, don't worry. It happens to all my live audiences until they understand the point. To begin with, first realize that it's not about the triangle in any way, shape or form. You can't do anything to the triangle to make it a circle.

It's at this point where people usually say, "You stop being a triangle."

That's half right. However, if you stop being a triangle, that doesn't make you a circle, does it? So if you're a triangle and you want to be a circle and you can't change the triangle, what do you do?

There is only one answer to that question. Think of it this way. If you're a baseball player and you want to be a football player, how do you be a football player? Is that a little more obvious now? You can't do anything to the baseball player to make him into a football player by working on his baseball game. Being a baseball player with shoulder pads and a helmet is not a football player either. You have to completely change the game. You have to BE a football player. It is the same for everything else. Being a triangle with rounded corners is not a circle. So, the only way to be a circle if you're a triangle is to BE A CIRCLE.

Now let's relate that to your life.

- If you're broke and you want to be rich, the only way to be rich is to be rich.

- If you're overweight and you want to be fit, the only way to be fit is to be fit.

- If you're unhappy and you want to be happy, the only way to be happy is to be happy.

- If you're unsuccessful and you want to be successful, the only way to be successful is to be successful.

Fill In Your Own Blanks

- I'm_____ and I want to be _____, the only way to be_____ is to be _____.

- I'm_____ and I want to be _____, the only way to be_____ is to be _____.

- I'm_____ and I want to be _____, the only way to be_____ is to be _____.

Now please understand what you can do with this exercise if you really take it to heart.

- In any moment, you can change your mind and start to be what you want to be
- You can inspire yourself to take immediate action
- You can empower yourself immediately
- You can motivate yourself at will
- You can begin attracting what you want rather than what you don't want

You see, you could spend the rest of your life working on all your stuff (working on your triangle) and you'll never be a circle. So many people get stuck in that loop of failure. They keep working on what they think and believe to be wrong and all they do is end up with more of the same. That is a never ending, futile search to fix the unfixable. Don't get caught in that trap. Stop working on what you think is wrong. Start working on what is right.

The Power Of Be, Do And Have

Who you are being dictates what you do. What you do ultimately dictates what you have. Start being who you want to be and doing what you want to do and then you'll be able to have what you want to have.

In other words, if you're BEING success minded, that will lead you to DO successful things and then you will HAVE what a successful person has. The reverse is also true. If you're BEING failure minded, that will lead you to DO what a failure does and you will HAVE what a failure has.

Now the 'Be, Do, Have' concept is great, but it won't change anything until you answer the following question. What determines who you are being?

There are three things that determine who you're being. The first is your unconscious beliefs and perceptions. You've now seen a great deal of them if you did the work diligently in chapter one. The second is pain and pleasure. You now know what you associate pain and pleasure to and how those associations motivate or demotivate you. The third thing that determines who you are being is your values. You'll get a chance to work on your values in chapter eight.

A Few Closing Responsible Thoughts

Will it be easy for you to be responsible in all the areas you haven't been? Probably not. Will it be comfortable? Certainly not! Will it be scary? Maybe. Will it be challenging? Absolutely. Will it be rewarding? Most definitely! You have a great many choices ahead of you and many more decisions. Being responsible to yourself and your desires will take you on a most magnificent adventure for the rest of your life.

"With great responsibility comes great power."
– Darshan G. Shanti

Summary Of Key Ideas And Important Points

1. You're responsible for everything whether you want to be or not.
2. Your number one responsibility is to yourself.
3. You are priceless.
4. Your life will work or not to the degree you are responsible.
5. The ego is your friend but it must be trained and you must be its leader.
6. At any point, you have the power to change your mind about who you are, about what you want, about your future, about your life.
7. Your decisions are based on either avoiding pain or gaining pleasure.
8. Your decisions move you closer to or take you further away from what you want.
9. You can use pain as a motivator, not as something to avoid, but as something to embrace.
10. Your life is ultimately, completely, definitely and unquestioningly in your hands.

CHAPTER 4

BECOMING CONGRUENT –
A FRONT AND REAR END
ALIGNMENT

"Your life changes the moment you make a new, congruent
and committed decision." – Tony Robbins

How well does a car run when it's out of alignment? Not too well. It pulls to one side; it wears out that side's tires and it's hard to steer. How well does anything work that is out of alignment? That includes you and your life. When you are incongruent (you say one thing and do another) it has a very strong, negative effect. If you think of a scale and you have many incongruencies in one area, one side of the scale will be weighed down.

The way I can best describe congruency is by its opposite. What congruency is *not* helps you to understand what it *is*. In other words, where incongruencies exist, the opportunity to be congruent becomes apparent. To illustrate, if you say you want to quit your job and start your own business and you've been saying it for umpteen years, but you still don't do it, that's incongruent and it's obvious what you need to do to become congruent. Simply do what you say you are going to do.

You shouldn't use congruency to punish yourself, but as a guidance system to let you know when you are on or off course. It is easy to see when you're off course. Just look at the results you have in your life. If you're not where you want to be and you keep making the same excuses over and over again, there is incongruency. In addition, check in with how you feel. If you are not satisfied, fulfilled or happy, that will also give you a clue.

The good part is that with every incongruency comes a gift; an opportunity to heal that part of you that needed to create the inconsistency in the first place. Napoleon Hill says, "Within every adversity lies the seed of an even greater benefit."

What Causes Us To Create Our Incongruencies

There are four things that cause you to be incongruent; your unconscious beliefs, what you associate pain/pleasure to, your perceptions and your paradigms. As I've talked about already in chapter one, your unconscious beliefs dictate what you do in your life. It's not what you know about your life that runs it. It's what you don't know. And you can't change what you don't even know is there. So if for example, you say you want to be fit but you find yourself eating poorly, too much, etc., that's incongruent. Now, what causes that incongruency is an unconscious belief. That belief may be something like, "I'm fat." "I don't deserve good things." "I'm not that important."

What you associate pain and pleasure to also creates incongruencies. If you want to be fit, but the immediate satisfaction and instant gratification of that big dinner and dessert is there, if you're incongruent, you'll eat the food. Simply put, it's more pleasureful to have the food and more painful to not have it. So, you find a way to reason with yourself that you can eat whatever you want and it won't cause you any problems or that you can eat whatever you want and still lose all the weight you want. The incongruency is a lie. The incongruency is a justification, an excuse, a reason you come up with to not be responsible. Once again, being responsible about being irresponsible is still irresponsible and it's also incongruent.

Your perceptions (first impressions) cause incongruencies as well. What you see is not what is. How you label yourself, your family, your friends, your job, your coworkers, your kids, your spouse, etc., is not reality and it's not the truth. It's just how you label those things. So, if you see yourself as a certain way, your actions will tend to be in alignment with your perceptions of yourself. Once again, how you see yourself is dictated by your unconscious beliefs. In chapter one, you did an exercise on how you developed your identity. The purpose of that was for you to get to as many negative, core beliefs about yourself as you could find. It is those core beliefs that are sponsoring the rest of the challenges that you may be having in your life.

The Power Of Paradigms

According to Joel Barker and Thomas Kuhn, paradigms are sets of rules and regulations that establish boundaries and enable you to be successful within those boundaries. They screen all of the incoming messages and allow you to see what you expect to see and filter out the rest. The more unexpected, the more difficult the information is to see. In other words, paradigms keep you from seeing what is actually there. They blind you with what you already know. Sometimes paradigms block you from seeing something that may be right in front of your eyes. Sometimes people will even go so far as to change the information they are seeing so it matches their paradigms. Paradigms enable you to see best what you're supposed to see and poorly or not at all what doesn't align with them.

For example, have you ever lost your keys and searched for them for hours? You finally give up and call a friend for help. When the friend came over, immediately she found the keys sitting on the kitchen table where they have been all day. Now you looked and looked and looked at that kitchen table and you would have bet your life they weren't there, but they were. It illustrates the point of paradigms that I am referring to. You didn't expect to see the keys there because something in you believed they were somewhere else. Your paradigm wouldn't let you see the keys because they weren't supposed to be there.

Another example of the power of paradigms is this. If you unconsciously believe you're fat, the scale has to read fat. Regardless of what weight you are, to you it will be fat. That way your beliefs and your reality are the same. That is why anorexic people see themselves as fat when they are wafer thin. It doesn't even matter what you say consciously, because the unconscious wins every time. There are no exceptions. The reason is that your unconscious mind and your conscious mind have to match. They have to be congruent because it keeps you sane and it also makes the world make sense.

Some major examples of paradigms that affected the world were:
- The world is flat
- The Earth is the center of the solar system
- Slavery
- Hitler's final solution
- Atomic/nuclear power
- The Swiss Watch manufacturers in 1968

Paradigms have both a negative and a positive effect.

On the negative side, they can:

- Stop change
- Keep you from saying yes to new ideas
- Paralyze you
- Make you think you know what's best & that your way is the only way
- Make moving ahead arduous and slow

On the positive side, they can:

- Show what's important and what's not
- Allow us to focus our intention
- Help us to find problems and then they give us the rules to solve them
- Help us stretch way beyond what we thought was possible
- Help us to be much more trusting

In truth, I could write an entire book on this subject, but there's no need to. If you want to learn more about paradigms, read Thomas Kuhn's book, <u>The Structure of Scientific Revolutions</u>. He was the first person to really bring this subject to the forefront and is the one the best resources on the subject. Another great resource is Joel A. Barker. His book is called, <u>Discovering The Future: The Business of Paradigms</u>.

Incongruency Reigned And We All Got Wet

I am about to share many examples of how pervasive incongruency is. None of them are meant to be negative or a scathing commentary on our world or any particular group. In addition, not all members of a group I mention are incongruent. I am simply pointing out these areas in order to help convey my point that being incongruent is devastatingly painful and deceitfully devious and serves to undo the moral fabric of humanity. It is not the focus of this writing to discuss the moral implications or the rightness or wrongness of some of these events that I point out, but rather just to show the inconsistencies. In addition,

I will share some very personal incongruencies in my life and how they caused so much pain and suffering that they almost destroyed me. It is my hope that reading these stories will have a deep, profound, lasting and transformative effect in your life. In so doing, you can learn from my mistakes, avoid my pitfalls, cut your learning curve and make some immediate changes in your life so you can have the life you've always wanted much quicker and easier.

The Salespeople

Have you ever met someone who was trying to sell you something and you knew that the person didn't believe in what he was selling? In other words, he wasn't a product of the product. For example, a 400 pound, rotund guy selling health club memberships. It just doesn't work. How about a doctor who preaches to you about quitting smoking and then goes and lights up on his break? What about a nutritionist who had Twinkies and soda for her lunch? What about a dentist who had rotten or rotting teeth? Something is off with that. It doesn't add up. It's out of sync. It doesn't feel right. It's incongruent.

When you see these people, you're automatically turned off. Your red flag meter starts to rise and you avoid them. You don't associate with them or want to do business with them. You may not be able to put your finger on it exactly, you just know that if you get involved with them, it's not going to work. If you go against that, you will pay a price.

If a salesman is incongruent, his credibility comes into question. Do you want to buy a Lexus from a guy who can't even afford to buy a Pinto? If his life is a mess, no matter the message of success he preaches, it won't matter. That was certainly true for me. My life was a mess and I was preaching success. Even though I said all the right words to everyone, they didn't sign up to work with me.

My darling Ajanel said to me one day, "No one wants what you have." Because of my paradigm, I couldn't hear that. I thought she meant that no one wanted personal development. I knew that wasn't true because personal development is a billion dollar industry. What she was saying that I couldn't hear was that no one wanted the lifestyle that I was living. Here I was speaking a great game, but living the opposite. I could make everyone else's life work, but I couldn't make my own life work.

Relationships

Couples often are incongruent. They have an unconscious agreement that says something like, "You don't call me on my stuff and I won't call you on yours." They use each other to be irresponsible. One smokes three packs a day and the other is a drunk. The wife can't tell the husband to quit drinking because she's worried about his health. If she did, how far do you think that would go? It would cause a huge fight with both of them defending themselves, their decisions, their irresponsibleness and their lies. And how about couples that have been together for ten or twenty years? How much weight have many of them gained?

Teachers

Many teachers are incongruent. I have seen countless teachers who don't give a hoot about their jobs or the young generation they are supposed to be inspiring. They are resigned, cynical and turned off. They just go through the motions doing as little as they can. Some of them have told me directly that the only reason they became teachers was because of all the time off they get. What does that teach the children? Even if just 10% of the teacher population is like that, many hundreds of thousands of young people's lives will be affected negatively.

Politicians

How many campaign promises do they make compared with what they actually deliver when they're elected? How many times do they do the exact opposite of what they say they're going to do? How many of them make laws and are then found guilty of breaking them? How many of them talk about the sanctity of the family and then go have affairs? The problem in being incongruent is that we don't believe what they are saying. We are turned off. We become resigned and cynical. We lose faith in them. We stop trusting them. In turn, we stop voting because we believe it won't make a difference. Not everyone will do that of course, but the many who do have an effect. What if we start to believe that nothing we do is going to matter? Then what? What if you start to believe that nothing you want to do is going to matter because you've been incongruent in so many areas for so long? It doesn't paint a rosy picture of your future, does it?

The Religious Institutions

Some of the people who run or ran our churches are incongruent. Take Jimmy Swaggart for example. He was extremely incongruent. While preaching the word of God and speaking of righteousness, he was a regular client of the prostitute Debra Murphree. At the same time, he unleashed fire and brimstone against rival TV evangelist Rev Jim Bakker for committing adultery with his church secretary Jessica Hahn. According to Wikipedia.com, following a 16-month Federal grand jury probe, Bakker was indicted in 1988 on eight counts of mail fraud, 15 counts of wire fraud and one count of conspiracy. In 1989, after a five week trial which began on August 28 in Charlotte, the jury found him guilty on all 24 counts. Judge Robert Potter sentenced him to 45 years in federal prison and a $500,000 fine. Jim spent about 5 years in prison in total.

Finally, how about the Catholic Church sex scandal? How many children were molested by these supposed "men of God?"

Parents

My dad used to tell me all the time, "Don't do as I do; do as I say." I would watch what he did and do what he did, not what he said. How many parents punish their children for cursing, yet they themselves curse up, down, right and left? How many of them get mad at their children for having bad manners, yet their own manners are atrocious? How many of them smoke, drink, lie, steal, yet punish their kids for doing the same thing? The point is, they say one thing and do another. Those incongruencies send conflicting messages to their children. In turn, the children get confused, lost and often follow the same paths as their parents.

Some Miscellaneous Incongruencies

Why do we teach children in school to talk about their problems and solve them through peaceful means, yet our countries go to war?

Why does our government spend hundreds of billions on war and then says it has no money to pay its teachers and its other public servants and institutions?

How about doctors and nurses who carry an extra 50 to 100 pounds and smoke?

What about the police who become criminals by beating their arrestees, stealing and tampering with evidence and who have sex with prostitutes?

What about prison guards who bring drugs to the convicts or have sex with them?

What about abortion and the death penalty? We, as healthy adults are not allowed to commit suicide. That's against the law. I assume because whoever made the law believes that life is precious. However we can kill people legally (Capital Punishment) if we want to and it's perfectly justifiable. As the bumper sticker asks, "Why do we kill people who kill people to show that killing people is wrong?"

How about the events that occurred at Abu Ghraib prison? What was done to some of those prisoners was incongruent with the Geneva Convention. Some may say they deserved it. Some may say they didn't. The point is that covering a prisoner in a 'brown substance' (possibly feces) or making one of them masturbate publicly or beating them while they were restrained or attacking them with dogs is incongruent with how a prisoner is supposed to be treated according to the Geneva Convention. Again, this is not a question of whether they deserved it or not.

Here's where it gets even deeper. I saw a lady on a talk show who is an alcoholic living in complete denial. She has cirrhosis of the liver and hepatitis C and was told that if she quit drinking she'd be put on the liver transplant list. A transplant is the only thing that will save her life. Do you think she quit drinking? Of course she didn't. The question then becomes why? Why was dying to her more pleasurable than living? And, how much pain was she in that she couldn't bear to be with even for a moment without her band-aid in a bottle? And, what do you think she thought of her own value? She was in denial of everything in her life. Even when she would admit what she was doing, she was denying. She would say things like, "I'm trying to quit." "I'm trying to get help." "I'm trying." She was so incongruent on so many levels and no matter how much pain she was in, it did not matter. To her, becoming congruent would be more painful. Because of that, she refused to take responsibility for anything, no matter what her family, the audience or the talk show host told her. Her denial was a survival mechanism that, quite ironically, was killing her. And she was powerless to change it or stop it. If she were to stop drinking, then what? How would she be able to handle her life? She had been drinking for over thirty years. She doesn't know any different. Her drinking saved her from the pain of the reality she didn't want to face, feel or experience.

I've had friends drink themselves into oblivion. I know people who have hundreds of pounds to loose...OR DIE. I know people who have cancer and still smoke. I know people who have the worst cases of diabetes you can imagine and you would think they would maintain the healthiest diet in the world and exercise rigorously and consistently. But they do the exact opposite. They eat all the crap they can, lie about it, gain weight, buy bigger clothes and tell people how much weight they've lost.

The point is that people will fight like hell to stay where they are, to stay in their comfort zone, to stay with what's familiar, to stay with what's known... EVEN IF IT IS KILLING THEM. They are surviving at the cost of their lives. Said another way, they are killing themselves to survive. That leads to the biggest incongruency of them all. It is not loving yourself. Ask your friends and your family if they love themselves. Most of them will look at you like you've been smoking some good stuff.

Why would anyone not want to love themselves? If you haven't figured it out by now, once again, it's the unconscious beliefs they formed as children.

How To Discover And Transform
Your Own Incongruencies

Start by asking yourself where you're incongruent. Take a look at your life. List all the areas where you say you want something and yet you do something else. Look at your health, your diet, your fitness, your relationships, your emotional life, your stress levels, your occupation, your success, your failure, your money, your happiness, etc. To help you do this, go back to your life satisfaction survey and you'll find plenty of ideas there. Then write down your excuses as to why you don't have them. You can do that very easily by putting two columns on a sheet of paper. The column on the left is where you list what you want. The column on the right you is where you list why you don't have it. Below is a template for you to use.

Incongruency Finder

The key here is to look at all of your excuses and see if there is a pattern to them. There are two types of excuses, internal and external. Internal excuses are caused by the beliefs you have about yourself (I'm not good enough; I'm unworthy; I fear success or failure). External excuses are caused by the beliefs you have about something outside of you such as, there's not enough money; there's not enough time or there's not enough support. The reasons that people don't have what they want in their lives are as numerous as the stars. Just think about how many excuses you've given yourself about why you haven't done what you said you wanted to do.

So if you have noticed a pattern, start digging. Keep asking yourself why. Every time you get an answer to that question, ask another. In a very, very short while you will arrive at the sponsoring belief. In most cases, it will be a personal one that you've been hiding from the world and from yourself. This is where the real magic of transforming your life and your paradigms comes in.

What I Want

1. _____

2. _____

3. _____

4. _____

My Excuses

1. _____

2. _____

3. _____

4. _____

BECOMING CONGRUENT – A FRONT AND REAR END ALIGNMENT

5. _____   5. _____

6. _____   6. _____

7. _____   7. _____

8. _____   8. _____

9. _____   9. _____

10. _____   10. _____

Let The Digging Begin

Most excuses sound like one of the following. These are the surface level excuses. These are the excuses we give ourselves and others over and over. They sound valid and justifiable and some of them may even be true. Regardless of the fact that they are true or not, excuses are just that. Many people think that having a good excuse is the same thing as doing what they said they would do. It's not. You either do what you say or you don't. There is no third option.

If any of these ring true for you, your excuses have got you.

- I'm tired
- I don't know what to do
- I don't know how to do it
- I've got to pay the bills
- I don't know the right people
- I don't want to make anyone mad
- I don't want to lose my friends
- I don't like change or the unknown
- It's too much work

- It will be too hard and too painful
- My spouse doesn't support me
- I don't have time
- I can't
- I might screw it up
- It's not that important
- It can wait
- I don't want to

To those excuses, I say, SO WHAT - NOW WHAT! In fact, you can use that expression in your life. When something comes up that would normally stop you, just say, "So what! Now what?" The 'so what' part dismisses the excuse and all the old beliefs and emotions and the 'now what' part propels you forward into a bright and open future.

Nothing great was ever accomplished by a bunch of tired, irresponsible, lazy, broke, unmotivated people... and nothing ever will. Now let's get a little more real. If we dig down and take those excuses to a deeper level, they may sound like this:

- I'm afraid to fail
- I'm afraid to succeed
- I'm afraid of what *they* will think
- I'm afraid to let people down

So, let's take these excuses down to the deepest level. These are the excuses we do everything we can to hide from ourselves and from the world. It's really not fear that stops you from your dreams. Fear is nothing more than your ego's way of protecting you from discovering that the core, negative beliefs you have about yourself are true.

So, I'm afraid to fail becomes the internal excuse, "I am a failure."

I'm afraid to succeed also becomes, "I am a failure." because a fear of success is the same thing as a fear of failure.

I'm afraid of what *they* will think becomes, "I don't love myself." because if you really loved yourself and knew you were priceless, it wouldn't matter what they think.

I'm afraid to let people down becomes, "I'm a disappointment."

The bottom line is that if you unconditionally loved yourself and knew that you were priceless, those beliefs would not exist and neither would your incongruencies. So take a look at all of your excuses. Go deep. Go to the core. Admit what you don't want to. Do it now. No one will know. It's just you and this book. When you find them, own them. The moment you do that, you're free. When you OWN your stuff NOW you will have WON.

Now I realize that most people will not actually do that exercise. They may give it slightly more than a few seconds of attention. Why? Because it is painful to look at what has been so out of whack. People think that it will be too hard, too much work or too painful to change. That's just their paradigm. It's just their perception. It's just in their imagination that it will be painful. It's only painful if they want to make it painful. And once again, what's at the root of it all is your unconscious beliefs. Keep digging away and soon you'll be liberated from them. Their roots may be strong, but you're stronger. You just have to want all the pleasure that's on the other side more than you want to stay comfortable now. Avoiding the pain you think you'll experience by looking at all of your incongruencies just keeps the pain around.

My Own Incongruencies

With all that said, I must now look at myself and share my own incongruencies. I am the microcosm for the macrocosm. My concern in sharing my 'humanness' and my past mistakes with you is that you will let it get in the way of your growth and you will make judgments about me and then let those judgments affect what you do with your life. If you decide to do that, so be it. It is your life. You may do with it as you wish. I am not responsible for your perceptions.

It is my hope (just as it has been in every chapter and will continue in the rest of the chapters) that in sharing, openly and honestly my weaknesses, my faults, my problems and of course, my incongruencies, that you can learn from them and go to work on your own. If you do that, you will not only heal yourself, but you'll help to heal many people around you as well.

I am incongruent in several areas of my life. I make no bones about that. I don't have it all figured out. I do not claim to be perfect or better than anyone, nor would I want to be. I don't want to be put on a pedestal because I can never live up to people's expectations of who they think I should be. However, I am in the process of becoming as congruent as I can be because my life absolutely stinks when I'm incongruent. It no longer serves me to be incongruent, know it and not do anything about it. That in itself, would be a major incongruency. I believe that becoming congruent is a lifelong process. I am in that process. In most cases, I am quite far along (between 80 and 95%) Please understand that what I am sharing with you is as real as it can be because it is raw, uncensored, unfiltered and I am experiencing deep emotions as I am writing. I am sharing exactly how I feel as an open declaration of what I have been covertly hiding. And it's not OK anymore. I am not denying it anymore. I am dealing with it. In this moment that I decide to own it, it can't own me anymore.

I talk about unconditional love for yourself and others, yet my love for myself and others has been conditional. It is hard to come to grips with that. As I write that statement, I feel nauseated, disgusted and pathetic. As I think about that, who am I to ever judge anyone, let alone me? Why would I have had the need to judge? What purpose did it serve in my life? Well the answer to that lies in the fact that I didn't unconditionally love myself. If I judge others and myself, I get to stay separate from everyone. Why would I want to stay separated from people? Yep, it's come full circle here. Because I didn't fully love myself. The reason I didn't unconditionally love myself was not very obvious. I just took it for granted that what I believed about myself was true. My guess is that you do the same thing. However the reason was that somewhere in the deep recesses of my consciousness I believed I was a bad person and therefore I couldn't love myself because I didn't deserve it. Do I still believe that? No.

I talk about forgiveness, yet it took me years to forgive some people and most importantly, myself. That too is disgusting. If I hold a grudge, once again I can separate myself. It brings tears to my eyes. And since forgiveness is a moment by moment gracious gift that I give to myself, I will keep forgiving myself until such time that I don't need to anymore.

I talk about responsibility, yet I've been quite irresponsible when it came to my health. As of this writing, (December 17, 2008) I am about 35 pounds overweight. I got that way by an injury I had while training for a marathon. I couldn't lift my knee more than an inch or two off the ground for almost a year. The irresponsibility came because I continued to eat as if I was still training. I ate very poorly as well. I made all kinds of excuses to help me feel better about being irresponsible. The point is that I loved food more than I loved being healthy and fit. I was avoiding the pain of denying myself what I wanted to eat. Being incongruent in this area stops me on many subtle levels. However, as I have come to see in so many areas of my life, once I make up my mind, it becomes easy. The congruent decisions are to be healthy, to eat right, to be fit and to treat myself like the priceless person I am. I now go to the gym 3 to 5 days a week and am getting back in shape. Keep in mind, I am doing this because I am no longer interested in dishonoring myself, in disrespecting myself, in hurting myself. It hurts me to even consider that.

I talk about honesty, yet I have lied to myself on many occasions. I've told myself all kinds of stuff that isn't true. I've said that I'm not good enough to make a difference all over the world. That's a bunch of nonsense. I've told myself I don't know how to go about doing that. Another lie. I've told myself that I can't really live the life of my dreams. I've told myself (my survival decision) that I'm unnecessary. It's all B.S. (Belief Systems). The truth of me is love. The truth of me is beauty, magnificence, greatness, wonder, love, light and joy.

I have been a coward. I have been afraid to speak and live my truth. I have been afraid to pursue my loftiest goals and have been afraid to be the greatest idea of the grandest vision of myself. As I close my eyes and see that future, it is totally unacceptable. It's not worth it. I don't want to be protected anymore. I am safe. The truth is that I can do anything I want. The truth is that my possibilities are unlimited and my future is an unwritten miracle just waiting for me to step into it.

I talk about being real, yet I have worn masks and pretended to be who I was not. That one alone caused more pain in my life than virtually all the rest combined. I have spent years doing all the right things and saying all the right things, but being someone who didn't believe what I was teaching to be true for me. As a result, my life was a constant struggle, full of pain, stress, anxiety, confusion. In short, I was a hypocrite. Yet none of this was intentional because it wasn't conscious. Now that it is conscious, it's not that way anymore.

The point is, I am either moving closer to, or taking myself farther away from what I want at all times. In every area where I am incongruent, I am taking myself farther away. I am hurting myself and I am hurting those around me. It is of course, the same with you.

My Mirror... Your Reality

After reading about me in all of those areas, what did you learn about yourself? Did you see yourself in my reflection? If so, was it painful? Was it encouraging? Are you beginning to understand what being incongruent in any area of your life costs you?

We must work on our own incongruencies in order to heal ourselves. We must look deep into ourselves in order to heal. It is in the admission, rather than the omission of our incongruencies that we free ourselves.

Transformational Questions

1. What is your definition of congruency?

_____

_____

2. How do you define congruency specifically in your life? In other words, fill in this blank. I am congruent in my life when...

_____

_____

_____

_____

3. **Where in your life do you say one thing and do another?** Don't be afraid to list as many as you can. No one need ever know what you've written but you. If you are not fully truthful, the only one you hurt is you.

_____

_____

_____

_____

4. In what areas do you think your life is out of sync?

_____

_____

_____

_____

5. Does your life work better and do things flow smoother and do you feel better when you are congruent? Yes or No? _____Please explain why.

_____

_____

_____

6. Do you believe that to be very successful, you need to be congruent? Yes or No? _____ Please explain.

_____

_____

7. Can you think of someone you know who is congruent in his or her life and list what you like about that person?

_____

_____

_____

8. Do you want those qualities in your life? Yes or No? _____ Why?

_____

_____

_____

_____

9. Think of someone you know who is NOT congruent in life or someone you just plain and simple do not like and list what you DON'T like about that person?

_____

_____

10. What you don't like about other people is just what you don't like about yourself projected onto them. These are areas where you are out of congruency. List the top five areas of your life in which you are out of congruency. If there are more, write more.

1. _____

2. _____

3. _____

4. _____

5. _____

11. There is some decision you keep making that is keeping those incongruencies still in place. What is it? Don't say, "I don't know." Really look to find it.

_____

_____

12. Why would you keep making that decision or those decisions? You may have to think about this one for a while. There may be a tremendous pain you associate with being congruent and tremendous pleasure with being incongruent. In essence, you may think it serves you to be incongruent. I'll give you a hint. It's all about your survival.

_____

_____

_____

13. What are you going to do differently from now on to take responsibility for the areas you are out of congruency?

_____

_____

_____

"When you find the way, others will find you. Passing on the road, they will be drawn to your door. The way that cannot be heard will be echoed in your voice. The way that cannot be seen will be reflected in your eyes."
– Lau Tzu

A Closing Word On Congruency

Being congruent is sometimes much easier said than done. Being congruent in all areas of your life may even be the most challenging thing you'll ever do. Certainly it is a lifelong process that starts with the awareness and then moves onto the decision to do something about it. Then comes the realization and acceptance that you are responsible for all of it. And finally you have to commit to becoming congruent.

Summary Of Key Ideas And Important Points

1. Incongruencies are everywhere.
2. People sense incongruency in you even if you try to hide it.
3. To the degree you are congruent, your life will flow smoother.
4. To the degree you're congruent; you will be much, much happier.
5. Incongruencies are a gift. They quickly show you what's not working.
6. The biggest incongruency of all is not loving yourself.
7. The paradigms that affect your life positively or negatively are discovered easily by seeing a pattern in your excuses.
8. When you change your paradigms you will be much more congruent.
9. Paradigms show you what you really believe.
10. Becoming congruent is a lifelong process. Take it slow and steady.

CHAPTER 5

THE POWER OF COMMITMENT

"The quality of a person's life is in direct proportion to their commitment to excellence, regardless of their chosen field of endeavor." – Vince Lombardi

Until One Is Committed

Until one is committed
There is hesitancy, the chance to draw back,
Always ineffectiveness.
Concerning all acts of initiative (and creation),
There is one elementary truth,
The ignorance of which kills countless ideas
And splendid plans:
That the moment one definitely commits oneself,
Then Providence moves too.
All sorts of things occur to help one
That would never otherwise have occurred.
A whole stream of events issues from the decision
Raising in one's favor all manner
Of unforeseen incidents and meetings
And material assistance,
Which no man could have dreamt
Would have come his way.
W.H. Murray from The Scottish Himalayan Expedition

When I think about the power of commitment, I am reminded of the old saying, "A chicken is involved with your breakfast, but a pig is committed." Most people are chickens when it comes to commitment. There is a double meaning to that. First, they are too scared to commit at all. And second, they never fully commit to most of the things in their life. They don't commit fully to their dreams, their goals and their future. They half-heartedly make a little effort never intending to accomplish what they set out to do.

The question naturally becomes, why? Why do some people commit so easily and others never do? You will begin to find the answer to that question as you read the following stories that demonstrate, like virtually nothing else, the power of commitment. As you read them, look closely at your own life to see how they relate to you. Ask yourself what you would have done if you were in their place. All of the stories you are about to read are extremely strong examples of the power of commitment.

And Edison Said, "Let Their Be Light."

Thomas Edison, one of the greatest inventors the world has ever known, did over 10,000 experiments before he perfected the electric light. He had to succeed because he never gave up. He ran out of things that did not work. As a result, he had to find the solution. He labored for untold hours every day, never losing sight of where he was going and of the outcomes he wanted. This was a man who didn't understand the meaning of failure or of quitting. In fact, the way he framed his numerous failed experiments was that he was not a failure. On the contrary, he was successful at finding 10,000 ways to not create a light bulb. Can you reframe your "failures" like that? If you did, how much more would that add to your life? Edison patented 1,093 different items. Yet his school teachers said he wouldn't amount to much and that he couldn't learn. So after very little public education, (about 3 months in total) his mother took him out of school and taught him at home.

I can only imagine how different the world would be if Edison had not been committed. Do you have an invention inside of you that will make a difference in the world? Have people told you that you couldn't do something? Did you believe them? Did it stop you? If it did, there is probably a place in your heart, a sadness that exists because you feel like you let yourself down. Well, learn the lesson from Edison now and begin to take action on your dream. In chapter nine, we will help you with developing a solid action plan.

A Kentucky Fried Idea... That Almost Never Was

Colonel Sanders, the man who started Kentucky Fried Chicken, retired and was living on social security. His check was tiny and he didn't want to live on that paltry amount for the rest of his life. So he took an inventory of his life and his skills, talents and abilities and the only thing that he found that he really enjoyed was cooking. He realized he had a great chicken recipe and decided to take it to a restaurant and give it to them in exchange for a little piece of the increased profits from chicken sales. The restaurant said, "No. We've got our own recipe so we don't need yours." Undaunted, he went to another restaurant and made his pitch. They also said no. The next one said no as well. And the next and the next and so on and so on and so on. But the Colonel was committed. He believed in himself and in his product. He was going to succeed no matter what. Yet each restaurant told him no. He changed his approach each time and with each rejection, he became stronger. Colonel Sanders went to all the restaurants in his town and in nearby towns and was told 'NO' at each of them. So he traveled farther and farther away from home. In fact, he kept pushing on for over two years, traveling all over the country, while living in his car. Do you know how many no's he heard before he got his first yes? 1,009 That's not a typo. He got One Thousand and Nine no's before he got his first yes. Of course, if he would have heard a no at 1,009, he would have gone on.

Would you have done that? Most people wouldn't have. They would have given up after the first two or three rejections. They would have reasoned that it was not worth it and that their idea wasn't a good one or that the timing was off or that the economy was bad. In other words, they would have come up with some excuse to not stick to their commitment.

By the way, if you don't stick to your commitments, you were never committed in the first place. Commitments are all or nothing. There are no grey areas. If you're sitting down reading this, just be 99% committed to standing up. If you stand up, that's 100%. Being any less than 100% committed might as well be 0%. Please don't fool yourself into thinking it's not. You're either committed or you're not, there is no third option.

What you must realize is that you're always committed to something. If you're 99% committed to standing up, what you're really saying is that you're 100% committed to sitting and 0% committed to standing.

The truth is that it's easy to be a quitter. It's easy to make excuses. It's easy to take the path of least resistance. It's easy not to commit. Easy, maybe. Detrimental to your joy, happiness, freedom, fulfillment, satisfaction and wealth, definitely. Sylvester Stallone's story illustrates this point perfectly.

"Yo Adrian, I Did It!"

When he was a kid, he would go to the movies because they would help him escape from his daily life. He thought it would be a great to be an actor when he grew up so he could help others escape and inspire them as well. He was big into helping people overcome tremendous odds because that's what he had done with his life. To begin with, when he was born, he was pulled out by forceps which gave him that droopy mouthed look and his slow speech. I don't know personally, but I can imagine what his childhood was like.

When he got older, he started out going to get acting jobs. The agents told him he was stupid looking and no one would want to watch a dopey looking guy who talks out of the side of his mouth. He was thrown out by over 1,500 agents in New York. Some of those agents he went to nine times. He finally got his first acting job because he went to an agent and couldn't be seen by him because it was too late in the day. But Stallone's commitment was very strong. He never went home. He spent the night on the steps. The next morning when the agent arrived to find Stallone sitting there, he couldn't believe it. So, wanting to get rid of Stallone, he gave him a role as a thug that got beaten up. But it didn't get rid of him. In fact, it whet his appetite more. It made him hungrier and made his desire stronger.

But by this time he was starving. He didn't have enough money to heat his apartment. His wife was screaming at him every day to get a job. He wouldn't do that because he knew that would have killed his real hunger to be an actor. He knew that he had to keep his true desire going because that was his only advantage.

He went to the library to keep warm and found a book by Edgar Alan Poe. He became fascinated with him and how he inspired people, so Stallone started to write and write and write. Then he started writing screenplays. He wrote screenplay after screenplay and just one of them sold. It was called Paradise Alley. It sold for only $100.00.

Can you believe that? After all that work, all that pain, suffering and stress, he only got $100.00. To most people, that would have been the final blow. Not to Stallone. His belief in himself and what he wanted was too great.

He got so broke that he hocked his wife's jewelry. That ended their relationship. She hated him and divorced him. So now he's broke monetarily, but not mentally. He was divorced from his wife but not from his dream.

The lowest day in his life came when he decided to sell his dog because he couldn't feed him. His dog was the only thing that loved him unconditionally. He went to a liquor store and stood outside and tried to sell his dog for $50.00. A guy negotiated with him and knocked him down to $25.00. After that, he went home and sobbed. You can imagine how he might have really questioned his commitment at that point. But he never lost sight of his focus; he never lost sight of what he wanted most.

Two weeks later, Stallone was watching a fight between Muhammad Ali and a guy named Chuck Wepner, aka, The Bayonne Bleeder. The guy was all heart and would not quit. Truthfully, even if he were lucky, it should have ended by the second round, but it went the distance (15 rounds). Near the end of round 15, Wepner was knocked out.

Stallone was inspired. He went home and went to work on his next screenplay. That screenplay was Rocky. He was so inspired and excited that he wrote it in seventy-two hours straight. He hardly slept. He knew that this was it. This screenplay was his ticket. So he went out to sell it. All the agents said it was predictable, stupid and sappy. He wrote down everything they told him and he ignored it. Finally he met some men (Robert Chartoff and Irwin Winkler) who believed in the script and they offered him $25,000.00 for it. He said they could have it as long as he could play Rocky. They said, "No, you're a writer not an actor." So he said they couldn't have the script. But they really wanted it. So, they offered him $100,000.00, then 150, 175. Each time Stallone said no to their offer because they didn't want him to be Rocky. They wanted Ryan O'Neal, James Caan, Burt Reynolds, or Robert Redford to be Rocky. Keep in mind, Stallone was totally broke, starving, dogless and divorced at the time and was just offered $175,000.00. Can you imagine what he was thinking and what he told himself after that? His level of commitment to be an actor was unshakeable. Most people would have taken the money and run. Not Stallone.

He knew that if he had sold the script, he would have lost his hunger, his drive, his passion. My guess is that if he had taken the money, we would never have seen him again.

They called him a few weeks later and offered him $250,000.00 for the script. Once again he turned them down. They came back with a final offer of $360,000.00. He told them that they could have it as long as he was Rocky. They once again said no and so did Stallone. Now, if you think Stallone was crazy for turning down $125,000.00, he must have been absolutely bonkers to turn down $360,000.00. Or was he? What was most important to him was his dream, not the money. Do you have a dream inside of you that you would do anything for? If you do, may this story inspire you.

The movie producers finally compromised and agreed to let him play the lead. They gave him $35,000.00 and some points in the movie. An interesting side note is that it only cost one million dollars to make Rocky and at the time, it grossed over $200 million.

The first thing Stallone did was to go back to that store where he sold his dog, hoping that the man would frequent the place so he could buy his dog back. He waited there for three days. On the third day, the man came by with the dog. Stallone said that he wanted to buy the dog back. The man told him no. Stallone offered him $100.00 and the man said no. But Stallone was committed. He then offered the man $500.00 and the man still said no. He upped it to $1000.00 and the man said that no amount of money would be enough for him because the dog was not for sale. But Stallone was not a quitter. So he offered the man $15,000.00 and a part in Rocky. The man finally gave in and sold Stallone his own dog back. Now for you Rocky fans, the dog that Adrian gave him (Butkus) was his real life dog that he had just bought back.

Is your commitment to yourself and your success as strong as that? What's the difference between Stallone and you? What did he have that you don't? The answer to that is NOTHING. He was committed. He was passionate. He knew what he wanted and why he wanted it. He believed in himself and in his future. He was better than his circumstances. He was determined. He was willing to do whatever it took to succeed. The pain (for Stallone) to not be an actor was far worse than having no money, no wife, no dog, no heat, no food. He used the pleasure of being an actor to continue to pull him forward. His own comfort was not as important to him as his future. To him, acting was the most important thing. That's why he succeeded.

When your commitment is that strong, you'll most certainly have whatever it is that you desire. There are no exceptions to that. But as you read his story, did you feel your heart sink because you don't believe you're as committed as he is? Or did your heart palpitate with excitement because you realized that your dreams are just a commitment away? The bottom line is that you're 100% committed to your dreams or 100% committed to not reaching them. Which one are you? There is no wiggle room.

> "You're either 100% committed to success
> or failure. There is no third option."
> – Darshan G. Shanti

Eddie Murphy Laughed His Way Up

Eddie Murphy's rule for success was similar. It was not to have a plan B. He was so committed to his goal of being a comedian that he didn't even entertain any other possibility. There was plan A and plan A only. That means that once he set his mind on what he was going to do, he did it and he had no escape route; he burned all his bridges. In other words, he had to succeed.

No plan B? That's craziness to most people. Burn your bridges. Pure insanity. Yet that's what Stallone and Murphy did and look what happened. Going through life on the good ship, 'What If' will guarantee one thing. You'll stay anchored to the dock. You'll be thinking, what if my boat gets a hole in it? What if I run into rough waters? What if I get lost? What if this and what if that? Who cares? You can "what if" yourself and your dreams to death or you can commit, but you can't do both.

People who constantly play the "what if" game are afraid. They may have a fear of success or a fear of failure or a fear of looking bad, but they are afraid. We'll talk about removing fear at the end of this chapter. The point is, when you have no chance of going backward or staying where you are, you have to move ahead, even when the situation looks impossible as in the following examples.

> "I believe life is constantly testing us for our level of
> commitment, and life's greatest rewards are reserved
> for those who demonstrate a never-ending commitment
> to act until they achieve. This level of resolve can move

mountains, but it must be constant and consistent. As simplistic as this may sound, it is still the common denominator separating those who live their dreams from those who live in regret."
— Tony Robbins

His Commitment Healed The Deaf

Napoleon Hill, author of the world famous book, <u>Think And Grow Rich</u> had a son (Blain) who was born without ears or any internal hearing parts. He was x-rayed and had every test available at the time. The doctor's told Napoleon that Blain would be a deaf, mute. Napoleon wouldn't even listen to the doctors. He immediately challenged their medical opinion and stopped them before they could go on and on and on about how dismal his son's situation was. He told the doctors that there was no situation that he couldn't do something about, even if it was just change his attitude about it. He then told the doctors that Blain would have 100% of his normal hearing. Hill writes of this moment,

In my own mind, I knew that my son would hear and speak... I was sure there must be a way and I would find it... More than anything else, I DESIRED that my son should not be a deaf, mute... Somehow, I would find a way to transplant into my child's mind, my own burning desire for ways and means of conveying sounds to his brain without the aid of ears.

Against all logical reasoning and an 'impossible situation', he committed and went to work on Blain right then and there. He began to pray and visualize and with every fiber in his being he believed that Blain would have his normal hearing. Napoleon worked tirelessly on him for one year, then two, then three, then four years. And up until that point, nothing changed for Blain, or so he thought. One day Napoleon walked up behind him and snapped his fingers on Blain's left side. He turned in that direction. So Napoleon snapped his fingers again, this time on the right side. Once again, his son turned his head to the right. Napoleon repeated this exercise over and over and each time Blain turned. Napoleon took him to get his hearing checked. After all the tests, it was determined that Blain had 60% of his normal hearing. But that wasn't enough for Napoleon. He said his son was going to have 100% of his hearing, not 60%. Several years later, a company specializing in hearing problems heard of Blain's phenomenal story and they created a special hearing aid based on bone induction. When Blain wore this hearing aid, it gave him the other 40% of his hearing.

When you look into your own life, are any of the tasks you have ahead of you as 'impossible' as Napoleon's was? If so, there's good news. He did it and so can you. When a situation looks impossible, let it impress you, not depress you. But if you don't commit, you'll never get the chance because you'll never get to the place where your commitment is tested. **And it's only at the point where your commitment is tested that all the miracles start to show up**. In addition, you will experience some of the greatest feelings you have ever felt in your life. You will feel like you're on top of the world. You will feel 'right' inside. You will have a knowingness deep within you that is unshakeable. You will know that the impossible is possible. You will know that there is virtually nothing you can't do if you set your mind to it. I say virtually because you are not going to be able to start flapping your arms and fly no matter how committed you are. However, within the realm of all human potential and possibility, there are virtually no limits. The next story illustrates that quite well.

The Miracle Man

Morris Goodman, (AKA The Miracle Man) should have died instantly or at best, been a vegetable all his life after crashing his plane on March the 10th of 1981 and breaking his neck at C1 and C2. He was brought to the hospital with a very shallow pulse rate and very low blood pressure. The nurses were breathing for him. He was unresponsive to pain. He was unresponsive at all. The doctors said no one had ever survived a break in either one of those areas, let alone both. They believed it was a miracle that he was even alive and that fact alone would surely make medical history. His spinal column was crushed. His larynx was damaged so severely that he would never speak again. He suffered permanent nerve damage that caused his liver, kidneys, bladder and his diaphragm to dysfunction which meant that he couldn't breathe without a respirator and would never be able to breathe on his own again. His swallowing reflexes were damaged so severely that he would never be able to eat or drink again.

The doctors didn't believe he would make it through the night. But he did.

Now, at some point, Morris became conscious and realized what had happened to him. The only thing he could do physically was blink his eyes. But his thinking power was 100% intact. Right then and there, he committed himself. He said if his mind was that destructive, then it could be used as powerfully to heal as well. He decided on a specific day and date to walk out of the hospital. It would be Christmas of that year. After four months, he was talking and he was in an electric wheel chair. He was breathing on his own and had motor skills in his entire upper body. The medical staff asked him what his recovery goal was. He said to walk out under his own power on Christmas and his ultimate goal was complete recovery. The doctors told him he needed to be realistic and that he would never function anywhere near the level he once did. He said that he didn't care what the doctors thought. It was only if he started to believe what they said that he would have been in trouble.

Five months after his accident, he was walking with a walker. Each day he got stronger and stronger. Each month, he needed less and less help from the physical therapists or any mechanical aid.

Sure enough, nine and a half months after his almost life-ending crash, he did just what he was committed to doing. He walked out of the hospital without mechanical help of any kind on Christmas day.

His website has a clip of his movie. http://www.themiracleman.org/w_movie.htm

Now, if you're thinking, "He was just lucky," I would challenge that assumption. There was nothing lucky about his situation or the intense hard work he put into his recovery. It was all very deliberate. Do you think if he wasn't committed to his wellness he would have recovered? That may sound like a ridiculous question. Obviously he wouldn't have. And that's the point. It may take that level of commitment for you to achieve your dreams. His wellness was paramount. Nothing else mattered. It needs to be the same for you and the life you want. Are your goals that important? Is your happiness that important?

A Moment To Reflect

After reading all of those stories, it would be a good idea to take some time to reflect on them. In other words, don't read on just yet. Think about those stories as they relate to your life. What did you learn from them? How could you use them to inspire you? Jot some thoughts down. What's important is that you internalize the messages in these stories as they relate to you. It's not about how much you write. If you need more space, just go to another sheet of paper.

_____

The Ups And Downs Of Commitment

Commitment takes a strong desire. It will keep you going in hard times. Commitment sometimes takes faith as you may not see the fruits of your labor for quite sometime. And you may not have any evidence that what you're doing is going to work. Commitment takes trust. You have to trust yourself, your intuition and the process. Commitment takes a steadfast, unwavering belief. But commitment doesn't have to be hard work. It may be hard at times, but not all the time. It can also be a lot of fun. As I write this paragraph, it is 3:30 am, the morning of April 19, 2008. I am steadily writing away in my office while I am listening to my favorite music. No one forced me to get up. I did not dread coming in and writing. In fact, I had only been asleep for two-hours before coming in. The truth is, I couldn't wait to come in and start. Because of my commitment, I had been awakened with many, many ideas. I couldn't sleep. Nor did I want to. It was too exciting to stay in bed. It's like when you first fall in love with someone. You can't wait to be with that person. You can't stand to be apart. Your every thought is about that person. Sleep is irrelevant. It can and will be the same way for you when you commit to what you want.

Now, it is not my intention to send mixed signals about commitment, but there is downside to being so committed to something. What that downside is will be different for everyone. There were many downsides in Stallone's life, but he was willing to weather them. Did his wife get hurt? Maybe yes. Maybe no. There are no victims. Was he irresponsible? In some ways, yes. The point is that you can blind yourself from what's happening around you to the point of hurting yourself or others. If your commitment to your dream is so strong that it is causing you physical harm, you may want to find another way to accomplish it. And you may not. Once again, it is a judgment call that you'll have to make when that time comes.

In my case, I caused myself tremendous physical and emotional pain, but quitting would have been worse for me. So I pressed on.

So here are some things for you to think about.

Transformational Questions

1. **Would any of these stories been possible without commitment?** Yes or No? _____

2. **Do you think these people spent any time being victims?** Yes or No? _____

They knew they weren't powerless. They knew that they could and would achieve whatever they wanted as long as they believed (without a doubt) in themselves; in their abilities; in what they wanted and in where they were going. They knew that it wasn't what happened to them that made them who they were; it's what they did with what happened to them that made them who they were. And what carried them through all of their trials and tribulations, all of their doubts and fears? That's right. COMMITMENT.

3. **If they could do what they did, what could you do?** Don't just glance over this question with a quick, "I don't know." Or an answer like, "anything" because that would be meaningless. Really take a few minutes to think about what you could do if you really committed yourself. If a bunch of fear comes up, don't worry. We'll deal with that shortly. For right now, just begin to dream a little and begin to stretch your mind and open it to new possibilities.

   _____
   _____
   _____
   _____

4. **How do you define commitment?** I am not interested in the dictionary definition. As always, you must define it for yourself. It is in your definition that you might find some unconscious belief.

_____

5. Do you think commitment is necessary in achieving your goals? Yes or No? _____

6. If you don't think it's necessary, list the reasons why.

_____

7. If you do think it's necessary, list the reasons why.

_____

8. Do you commit to things you enjoy more easily than things you don't? Yes or No?_____

9. What positive associations do you have with commitment?

_____

What you just wrote is like both the spark that will ignite your flame and the fuel that will keep you going. It's these positive associations that you really want to focus on because that is what you will create. As Wayne Dyer says, "As you think, so shall you be."

10. **In what general areas of your life have you been making excuses and holding yourself back?** Take a look at your diet, your exercise, your health, your career, your family, or whatever area that's important to you.

_____

11. Where could you specifically step up to the plate in each of those areas and take responsibility for yourself and your dreams?

_____

_____

_____

_____

12. On a typical project that you do for your life or for your business, what is your level of commitment on a scale of 1 to 10? _____

13. If your answer is less than 10, why would you give less than 100% effort to something you've committed to? _____

_____

_____

Your answer should give you clues as to what is happening in your unconscious thoughts. If you said you're lazy, go deeper. If you said, "It's too much work," go deeper. If you said, "I wasn't really that interested," go deeper. Your goal here is to get to the core, sponsoring thoughts. So keep digging until you get to the deepest place you can go. This is where most people will get stuck and they will have a tendency to skip this question and say it's not important. It is important. Just keep asking why you've written what you've written. You will find an answer.

14. **What have you committed to in the past that you are still doing that no longer serves you?** Maybe you're hanging on to a romantic relationship that should have ended a long time ago. Maybe you're at a job you should have quit. Maybe you're hanging on to old beliefs about yourself.

_____

_____

_____

15. **Why are you still doing it?** This will help you to distinguish your unconscious fears. Take your time with this.

_____

_____

_____

Does it really make sense to keep doing what no longer works for you? Of course it doesn't. Yet if you are still holding on, it's unconscious. These answers are all leading you to discover your core thoughts and fears. Usually people are avoiding some type of pain and that pain is usually associated with a fear and that fear is related to what you made up about yourself and is now your identity. You can go back to chapter one and see what you wrote as your survival decision.

16. **What negative associations and fears do you have with committing to something and as a result it stops you from committing?**

_____

_____

_____

If commitment is too hard, too much work, too painful, too much responsibility, too constricting, too whatever, is it likely that you're going to want to commit to anything? Probably not. So we need to discover where your negative associations are coming from. As I alluded to earlier, they are based in your survival decision and that is where fear comes from. So let's take a deep look into fear right now.

Seeing Fear For What It Is And Removing It For Good

One of the best things that has ever been written about fear is from Marianne Williamson in her book, <u>Return To Love</u>. This quote is often erroneously credited to Nelson Mandela. He said it in his 1994 presidential, inaugural speech, but he was not the author. Anything you could read that is written by Marianne would make a wonderful difference in your life. She is a true gift to the healing of this planet.

Our Deepest Fear

Our deepest fear is not that we are inadequate.
Our deepest fear is that we are powerful beyond measure.
It is our light, not our darkness that most frightens us.

THE POWER OF COMMITMENT

> We ask ourselves, who am I to be brilliant, gorgeous,
> talented, fabulous? Actually, who are you *not* to be?
> You are a child of God. Your playing small
> does not serve the world. There is nothing enlightened
> about shrinking so that other people won't feel insecure
> around you. We are all meant to shine, as children do.
> We were born to make manifest the glory of God
> that is within us. It is not just in some of us;
> it is in everyone. And as we let our own light shine,
> we unconsciously give other people permission
> to do the same. As we are liberated from our own fear,
> our presence automatically liberates others.

If I were you, I would read that over and over and over again. I would dissect it and see how it fits in every area of your life. I would change the words so it is written in the first person (I Language) and commit it to memory. If you truly take on the wisdom in those words, you will move light years ahead of where you are now.

There are also some very good acronyms related to fear. You can remember them easily.

Foolish
Ego
Altering
Reality

Feelings
Escalated
Anticipating
Reality

Forget
Everything
And
Run

"Fear is that little darkroom where negatives are developed."
– Michael Pritchard

Here is a great way for you to understand how fear works and where it comes from. Think back to when you were in high school. Was there ever someone (who was available) that you wanted to go out with, but you didn't ask out? Chances are, the answer is yes. If it's no, just follow along and the point I'm making will become clear. Now, assuming you were available as well, why didn't you ask that person out? What most people say is that they didn't want to be rejected. In other words, they had a fear of rejection. It is at this point where I tell everyone that fear of rejection doesn't exist in any way, shape or form. They look at me like I'm crazy. I then tell them that I will prove it beyond the shadow of a doubt.

If you asked this person out and you were laughed at or just turned down flat out, what would you have told yourself about you? That's the critical part. It's not what you would have said about the other person, such as, "It's his loss." or, "She doesn't know what she's missing." It's what you would have said to yourself about you. So what did you tell yourself? Most people say something like, "I'm not good enough." Or "I'm unworthy." Or, "I'm not good looking enough."

Now here's where the origins of fear come together. Do you want anyone, let alone someone you're interested in dating, find out your core, survival decision that you're not good enough? Of course you don't. No one wants their core beliefs discovered, validated or challenged.

Let's take it deeper. If you know down deep that you're not good enough, you'll do anything to hide it from everyone, including yourself. Why? Because if "they" discovered that you really aren't worthy, your protection would be gone. Then what? If your core, negative beliefs are exposed, life becomes not very much fun anymore. Most of the people in my audiences tell me that life wouldn't even be worth living. What that means is that a fear of rejection is not a fear of rejection at all. It's a fear of discovery and validation that the deep, dark, negative beliefs you have about yourself are true.

By the way, that's what a fear of failure is as well. If you set a goal and go for it and you don't reach it, you may be labeled by them or by yourself as a failure. That automatically validates those negative beliefs. That's simply too painful to be with, so most people never really stretch themselves. They never have to risk looking like or experiencing the feelings of what they perceive to be failure.

I recently was told by a friend of mine that she would rather kill herself than to be a failure in her own eyes or in the eyes of others. She said her problem was that she didn't know who she was. As a result, she really didn't like her life. I told her that she did know who she was, but she was just afraid to be that person. I then asked her who she would be if she wasn't so scared. She rattled off, strong, independent, my own person. I said, "That's who you are." She was blown away. She was so busy being afraid of failing and not living her life to any high level, she was just existing, going through the motions, drifting along. There was no point, no purpose, no passion and no power to her life. The irony is that she was so afraid to fail that she was a failure. She attracted to her that which she gave the most energy to. Yet she was a failure without even going for anything big because to fail at something big would have been worse.

You can see how her fear stopped her. There was literally no way she could do anything different and therefore there was nothing she could commit to but to stay on the same path that was destroying her. Just like a moth to a flame, she was helplessly driven to her destruction. Said another way, her need to avoid failing set her on a course to her own failure. And her need to avoid failure was deeply rooted in her survival decision. Yet that same deep, intrinsic need was what was actually killing her. Failing to her, meant that her core, negative beliefs were true. As I said before, no one wants their core, negative beliefs validated because when they are validated, life is not worth living. This is the human condition. This is what stops people from living lives of their dreams. They don't want to ever even have it be possible that there is even a small chance that they would be discovered for who they really are. So, they lead lives well within the center of their comfort zones to make sure they stay safe at all costs. I call that a living death; survival at the cost of your life. And for some people, that's all they will ever be. But you don't have to be like that. Not for one minute more do you have to live that life. Make a new, empowered decision right now and commit to it. Will it be scary? Probably. Will it be worth it? Definitely!

A fear of success is virtually the same thing. It's just a fear of failure turned inside out, with a small twist. If you've had a fear of success for years and years and somehow you get to be a success in spite of it, what happens to you if you can't maintain that success? That's right, you may fail. Once again, if you fail, your core, negative beliefs (your survival decision) will be validated. That will make life really unpleasant at best and not worth living at worst and so you'll avoid success. Here's the twist. A fear of success is also about not wanting your core, negative beliefs challenged. For example, if you've had a fear of success for thirty-years and I come along and tell you that you can be a success immediately if you want to, you'll look back on your life over those years and say something to yourself like, "I've wasted the last thirty-years of my life believing I was a failure." That's very sobering and painful. So, the thought that it's too painful to be successful is what keeps many people from ever achieving huge levels of success.

A Closing Message About Fear

The debilitating effects of fear are on their way out of your life. They don't have to control you anymore. Right now you can make a decision that fear will not now or ever hold you back. It is completely up to you.

And, you might want to go over this section on fear again. It is so deep and has so much information, it may take a bit for you to wrap your head around it and really understand it and what it is doing to you. When you really under-stand it well, go on to the transformational questions.

OK, it's time for you to do some work on yourself so that you can directly experience on a deeper level what I am talking about here.

> "We can't fear the past. Fear is a future thing.
> And since the future's all in our heads, fear
> must be a head thing."
> – Tom Payne

More Transformational Questions

1. **What does fear mean to you?** That is, how do you define it for yourself? The object of this exercise is for you to really take a look at what fear actually is, instead of some nebulous concept. Some people have said things like, "Fear

is a darkness that never lets me see." "Fear is a monster that I can't ever defeat."

_____

_____

_____

_____

_____

_____

Now, if I asked 1,000 different people what their definition of fear is, how many different definitions would I get? That's right, I would get 1,000. Now if I would get 1,000 definitions, that means fear is completely made up based on the individuals' perceptions, thoughts, beliefs, etc. In fact, fear is really just a survival mechanism.

2. **What internal fears do you have?** For example, "I am afraid people will find out who I truly am." or, "I'm afraid to be disapproved of." "I'm afraid people won't like me." "I'm afraid I'll be abandoned." Etc.

    _____

    _____

    _____

    _____

Your internal fears will lead you to your core. Whatever you wrote, you must now take it to a deeper level. If you take "I am afraid people will find out who I truly am." for example, why would you be afraid that people will find out who you truly are? What's so bad about you that you wouldn't want people to discover it? What's so wrong with you in your mind that you couldn't even bear the thought of anyone knowing? If they did find out, what would that mean for you?

It's those questions that people are too afraid to confront. And it's because those questions are not addressed that people settle for far less than they could have or never go for what they want in the first place. That leads into the next question.

3. **What external fears do you have?** In other words, what have you not done that you truly want to do because you have been too afraid?

For example, "I have not gone for my dreams." or "I never opened my own business." Etc.

_____

_____

_____

_____

You have to be honest with yourself when you write the answers here. If you have a long held desire that you have never taken action on, write it down. To the degree that you're totally honest with yourself, you will be successful at putting your fears aside.

4. **Why? What were you afraid would happen to you if you did those things?** If you are tempted to say, "Nothing would happen." then you should ask yourself why you never did them in the first place. Now, in reality, nothing would happen, but in your mind, you believe something would and that is what stops you. In other words, there is some consequence you don't want to experience and/or there is some pain you want to avoid.

_____

_____

_____

_____

As I stated earlier, the pain you wanted to avoid was finding out that your survival decision is true. Does what you wrote agree with that statement? If it doesn't, keep digging.

5. **Do you know for sure those things you wrote down in question 4 would happen or are you just thinking they will and letting your thoughts stop you?** In other words, what evidence do you have that those things would happen?

_____

_____

_____

_____

"The only thing we have to fear is fear itself – nameless, unreasoning, unjustified terror which paralyzes needed efforts to convert retreat into advance."
– Franklin D. Roosevelt

The following section pretty much sums up the entire book to this point. Just like Marianne Williamson's quote, do yourself the favor and read this section over and over until you have internalized it. Dissect it and see how it fits in every area of your life. If you truly take on the wisdom in those words, you will move light years ahead of where you are now.

The following section is written in the first person (I language) so that as you read it, it will sink deeper into your consciousness. As I have come to observe and understand, this is the human condition in a nutshell

The Grand Irony Of Life

The grand irony of life is being afraid to be who I truly am for fear that life would not be worth living and that I will die because of the rejection I will face and the lack of love that I will experience. In reality, the exact opposite is true. Not being who I really am is what causes me to live a life of complete unfulfillment, dissatisfaction, pain, fear, sadness, weakness, helplessness, anxiety, stress, aggravation, boredom and victimization. That is no more than a living death, survival at the cost of my life.

The reason I am afraid to be who I really am is that it will mean my whole way of living, all my beliefs, thoughts, feelings, etc. will be instantly invalidated and as a result, my life would be over because there would be nothing left of me. All my excuses, my worries, my fears, my doubts, my anxieties will be gone. Then what? What would I do? Who would I be? The thought of that is terrifying. It is so terrifying that I never even entertain the concept, let alone consider that it's true for me. And since I don't know any different way to live and I have no concept of what my life would be if I wasn't making my excuses anymore, I am paralyzed. I stay exactly where I am.

The ultimate irony is that not being the real me is what is actually killing me. Slowly but surely, it sucks the very life out of me. It consumes me. It keeps me down and prevents me from ever believing or being anything else. It becomes my life. I become its victim. And I am powerless to ever change it because I don't even know it is there.

If I am the real me, I run the risk of not being loved, appreciated and valued. I run the risk of failing. I run the risk of losing what little I have. I also run the risk of having my core, negative beliefs about myself validated and that's way too painful. That's why I believe that if I am the real me, life will not be worth living. Somewhere down deep within my soul, I know that I can't live without that. The problem is that it's just external validation. I believe I need that validation to survive because I don't have it within me. That's the never ending game I play. So I spend my whole life pretending to be someone I'm not in order to stay alive and that's why I avoid being the real me at all costs.

That only leaves me with one decision, (that if I don't do) my life will really be over.

BE THE REAL ME!

Once again, if you would like, please go to www.the24hourchampion.com and click on the Templates tab, then click on 'The Grand Irony Of Life' and you can have a single page copy of that. Please feel free to send it to your friends and loved ones as well.

At this point, it should be pretty clear to you now what not being who you truly are is costing you. Right now you can make the decision to be the person you've always wanted to be, to do what you've always wanted to do and have what you've always wanted to have. Right now you can commit to yourself and your future. Right now you can commit to being a 24-hour champion. Right now you can commit to be the real you.

"Fear is a violent storm that dissipates the moment the sun comes out. You are the sun."
– Darshan G. Shanti

To close this chapter, I would like to share one of the 600 poems I have written. May it serve you and bless you. If you would like a full size copy as well, you can go to www.the24hourchampion.com and click on the Templates tab, then click on 'Never Let Fear Hold You Back Again.'

NEVER LET FEAR HOLD YOU BACK AGAIN

What is this thing we call fear?
Have you ever looked at it really clear
And taken it apart section by section
To see what was responsible for its conception?

You see, there is much more to the emotion of fear
Actually, it's based on some thoughts that really domineer
And take over your rational thought form
Until living that way becomes the norm

And you don't even realize that the fear is not real
Because it's such a strong emotion that sometimes it's all you can feel
And by that point it's too late as it has already got you
And there's no way out and nothing you can do

So if fear is consuming you completely
And no matter what you do, you still can't see
How to rid yourself of it and never again let it near
There are some things that must become clear

You must realize that you are always at choice
And that you don't have to listen to your ego's voice
You can master even the most intensely fearful emotion
All it takes is time and devotion

Please understand that fear is not your master and you are not its slave
But fear is tricky and will try to make you behave
It will try to keep you from living your power
It will make you want to bow down and cower

But it has no control over you unless you give it the chance
If you do, you become a victim of your own circumstance
As fear then takes over and is in control
And now you're stuck, frozen in a fearful mold

And that's the cycle that never stops and never goes away
Until you decide that it's a game you no longer want to play
And once you recognize fear for what it is and what it is not
Then all the power and all the freedom is what you've got

Summary Of Key Ideas And Important Points

1. Commitment is an all or nothing game...no plan B.
2. You're always committed to something.
3. Commitments are freeing not binding.
4. Your life works to the degree that you keep your commitments.
5. Your ultimate commitment is to be the real you.
6. Fear is made up. It's a tactic your identity uses to keep you surviving.
7. When you face your fear, it will disappear.
8. Fear has no power except that which you grant it.
9. There is no courage without fear.
10. Fear is a violent storm that dissipates the moment the sun comes out. You are the sun.

CHAPTER 6

TRUST YOUR GUT NO MATTER WHAT

"Intuition is the very force or activity of the soul in its experience through whatever has been the experience of the soul itself." – Henry Reed

The purpose of this chapter is to convey the benefits of living intuitively. I will do that partly by sharing my experiences of not living that way. It is my hope, once again, that you will take my example, learn from it and not repeat those mistakes yourself.

Writing this book has been a highly intuitive process. Since I learned to listen to and follow my intuition, my life has changed enormously… for the better and in every way imaginable. I am much happier, more fulfilled, healthier and wealthier and I'm much more 'alive'. I am proud to say that I am not a member of the Frank Sinatra club. I no longer have to do it "My Way" because I no longer have to be in control of everything. I can tell you this with absolute certainty. For the rest of my life, I will continue to listen to the wisdom of my intuition and follow its quiet, gentle and sometimes very challenging guidance. As a result, my life will be a miracle waiting to happen, not a mess, waiting for a miracle. Yours can be too, if you decide for it to be that way.

Any discussion of intuition could not occur without talking about God. Everyone has a different idea about what God is and is not, myself included. How I have decided to deal with that in this chapter is to call God by many different names. Some of them are: the Universe, Infinite Intelligence and Infinite Wisdom, yet it's all God. For those of you who don't believe in God, it makes no difference whatsoever. For those of you who have strong, fundamental religious beliefs, it also makes no difference as this chapter's information does not conflict with any belief or religion.

What Is Intuition?

In the countless books and articles that have been written about intuition, I have discovered that they all say virtually the same thing about it, but they say it in just a slightly different way. I am no different. You are about to read my take on it. Use what works for you and discard the rest. It is my intention that you will read the following pages and get a clear understanding of what it is, why it's important and how to use it.

Intuition is knowing and understanding without any evidence or knowledge that what you know even exists. It's not guessing. With intuition, you can know anything, anytime. It is an instant awareness. It is an internal knowing. Unlike traditional methods of gathering information, there are no linear steps. In other words, when you use your intuition, you can go from beginning to end, directly bypassing everything in the middle. By using your intuition, you can sense the unseen and 'feel' the universal energy that lies within us and all around us, dormant, waiting for us to come to it. In Latin, intuition means *in to you*. It is your divine, higher spirit talking to you. Intuition is the collective consciousness and it is the gateway to the infinite, to all that is, to the universal storehouse of knowledge, to universal wisdom, universal love and every other thing imaginable. Think of this Infinite Wisdom like the internet. All the information is available at the touch of a button. You can 'download' anything you desire in a virtual instant. Or you can just leave it where it is. You can follow the information that you are given or you can ignore it and do it your own way.

Intuition is the part of you that knows all, sees all and understands all. It is your god-self. It is your connection to all that is. It is the Universal Internet that is totally free and is on 24-hours a day. It is constantly sending its signals that never stop. It's subtle. It's quiet. It's familiar. But it disappears into your daily routine and you tend not to notice it. For example, if you put on a pair of dark sunglasses, when you first put them on, the world appears dark. But if you leave them on for a while, the world does not look dark anymore. It just looks 'normal'. Yet the dark information is being sent to you all the time, but you just can't 'see' it. You believe that what you are seeing is the reality, yet it is not.

The reason is that it has become part of your background information. In other words, it's not conscious. It becomes your paradigm.

Michelle Casto, in an article entitled,
What Is Intuition And How Do I Use It? says,

Intuitive messages range from an inkling to a strong sign or message. Your inner self is persistent and consistent. It will keep trying to get your attention until you finally wise up! An inkling is like a glimmer or passing feeling/ thought that comes from somewhere inside and usually precedes a hunch or intuitive message. A "hunch" is accurate information from a higher intelligence; therefore, you can rely on it. An intuitive message ranges from hearing actual words, seeing a clear picture, or a deep inner knowing. Some people experience intuition as a feeling, others a gut reaction, others will see images or have a dream, others hear an actual message. Become familiar with how your inner self communicates with you.

Intuition is also like a wise old mentor that will always be by your side waiting patiently, guiding you, supporting you, and gently nudging you. Like any good relationship, it takes communication. You need to be able to ask for what you want and you need to be able to listen to what it tells you. Like building any muscle, it will take time and attention for you to build it; that is, for you to understand its subtleties.

Why Is It Important?

Well, that depends on what kind of life you want in virtually any area. The following is just a tiny list of benefits. What is for sure is that:

• Your stress level will drop to virtually nothing

• You will say goodbye to worrying and anxiety as there will be no need for it

• You will feel better physically, emotionally, mentally

• You will be healthier

• You will attract people and circumstances that help you live your dreams

- You will sleep better due to so much less confusion and stress

- You will not fear success, failure or be afraid of taking risks

- You will be able to take action much more quickly

- Your attitude will be much better

- You will think much more clearly

I'll illustrate by sharing two instances in my life in which the consequences of not listening were so severe, it almost killed me.

I met this man who was brilliant. He could make money (and lots of it) at the drop of a hat. Anything he touched seemed to magically turn into wealth. He was charismatic, quick witted, extremely creative and very powerful. I saw a great deal of myself in him. He had qualities I wanted to develop more of in myself. He had a lovely wife and four beautiful young daughters all in elementary school. He appeared to be a good father. All the kids were well fed and seemed well adjusted. His wife had a good head on her shoulders and was a professional woman working for a respectable company as a manager. On the surface, things seemed to check out. His references were good. So, I decided to go into business with him doing radio advertising.

The problem was, as I soon found out, that he had no money. So, I began financing everything with my credit. Of course he promised to pay the bill when it came due (in full) because we were going to make so much money. He assured me over and over that I had nothing to worry about.

Through this whole process, something in me didn't feel right, BUT I IGNORED IT. After all, I wanted to make the money he promised. I was having fun. I was learning.

But with each new day, I had to do more and more and I had to buy more and more. My gut kept telling me that something was wrong. So many things just weren't adding up. But by this time, we already were making money. I was doing the selling of the radio spots and he was doing the radio show. In the beginning, all was good. He was doing the show and it was being played on the air. The commercials were recorded professionally and got played as promised.

But then, he started needing more and more money and everything I brought in was not enough to meet his needs. I kept selling the spots, but he stopped doing the show and recording the commercials. He kept promising me it was just a technical glitch and that soon everything would be fine.

It wasn't! In fact, it was about as bad as it could be. He was in so much financial trouble from all of his other bad dealings (which I had no conscious idea about) that he called me up one day and said that he was moving out of state with his family because he couldn't take the pressure anymore. I asked him to stay and help me take care of the debt and he said no. He actually called me because he wanted to relieve his guilt about moving, not because he wanted to help me. I know this because he had the unmitigated gall to tell me so.

He left me holding the bag. All of the people I sold those spots to who were not put on the air demanded that they get a refund immediately. I had no way to give them their money back. My partner absconded with all of the remaining money, spent the rest, sold all the equipment I bought and took off. As each one of them called me, I explained the scam I was caught in the middle of and that I was just as in the dark as they were. I offered to work the debts off to those who would allow me to. But that was all I could do.

I felt horrible. I was helpless. I was used and manipulated and my kindness was taken advantage of. I really screwed up by not listening to my intuition from the very beginning. It was telling me not to trust this guy. It was telling me not to pay for everything, but I thought I knew better. I ended up about $30,000.00 in debt when it was all said and done with no ability to pay for it. I filed bankruptcy and ruined my credit for ten years.

Even though my gut was screaming at me, I refused to listen. Even though there were a bunch of red flags, I was color blind. Even though, nothing added up, I didn't do the math. I ignored all the warning signs and did what I wanted to do. It was my ego trying to feel important. I felt as if I would be someone if I was successful. What I am saying is that I didn't listen to my intuition because I didn't have enough love for myself and belief in myself. The irony is that I knew my intuition was right. I just could not listen to it because I was too afraid of being nothing, of being a failure. I paid a very high price to validate that fear.

On a more positive note, when I listened to what my intuition told me, it changed my life immediately for the better. If I hadn't listened to it, you wouldn't be reading this book. I'll explain.

About eight years ago, I was working as a substitute teacher and had been for the previous year. I was writing an assignment on the board and I heard this voice loud and clear that said, "You don't need the safety of the classroom any-more. It's time to bring your gifts to the world." That voice was crazy. There was no way possible that I could or should have quit. I had no life coaching experience. I had no plan. I had no backup. I had no evidence that it would work. On top of that, I had no money. I was behind on my rent and virtually everything else. I started working two jobs for a total of 280 hours a month just to get caught up and keep current on my bills. I didn't even have one duck, let alone a bunch of them, to get in a row.

Yet as soon as I heard the voice, I instantly knew it was right. I couldn't argue with it. I just trusted it. So I finished subbing a few weeks later and started off on my own. I immediately got my first client from the second job I was working. I then got a corporate training job, then another, then another. Then I got a few more clients and the business started to take off. Clients were coming regularly. I was getting referred right and left. It was a great beginning.

Then I stopped listening to my intuition and everything started to fall apart. My clients started firing me. I was attracting clients who had no real intention of changing. I was attracting clients who wouldn't pay or couldn't pay. I was doing more and more every day just to stay afloat.

You may wonder why I would stop listening to my intuition. Well, I fell into the trap I am warning you not to fall into. My ego got in the way. It thought it new better and it could take control and do a better job. It bullied its way in and shoved aside its rival. My intuition offered no struggle and left the ego to do what it wanted. It failed miserably as it always does.

The point is that by not listening to my intuition, my business fell apart and my life and my health did as well. And when I did listen to it, life was easy, business was great and I was healthy.

Of course, it will be the same for you.

How Do You Listen To It?

The first thing that you need to do is to learn how to tune into the messages that are being sent. You have to learn how to pay attention to your feelings and your emotions. Your emotions are happiness, sadness, anger, etc., and can be described with words. Your feelings can't really be explained and are more like physical sensations in your body.

Something may just "feel right" or "feel wrong" about a situation. Your body may feel weighed down and sluggish if a decision you are about to make is wrong or it may feel light, free, peaceful and easy if it is the right decision.

For example, a salesman is trying to sell you some kind of widget and everything sounds great, looks great, but something "feels off." You can't quite put your finger on it. You just know that it's not quite right. You notice that when you think about buying the widget, your body feels heavy or you may have a knot in your stomach. Listen to what your body is telling you. It is your intuition screaming at you to not do what you're about to do. It's telling you to check into it more and to ask more questions and do more research. This is where most people go wrong. They feel that feeling and then they ignore it. Your intuition knows something you don't. It is warning you away from buying the widget for reasons you may not even be aware of consciously. As Lynn Robinson writes in her article, *4 Ways to Find Answers to Life's Questions Using Intuition,*

> Your intuition will provide you with information to make positive choices. Would it make sense for you to be sent to earth with a magnificent inner guidance system and every time you trusted it you felt awful? No!

Living Intuitively From This Moment On

What you are about to learn is not a technique, not a concept, not a tool, but rather a brand new, beautiful way to live for the rest of your life if you please. It is called, Surrender, Allow and Trust (SAT). It is intuition in action. It is quite simple, but not easy to do, sometimes. Yet, it will help you to change your life in immeasurable ways.

Surrender, allow and trust is the first step in creation. It is the art of being. We must be, before we do and we must do before we have.

I have learned how to surrender, allow and trust and how to live this way from my beautiful partner Ajanel. She shared this idea with me many years ago and quite honestly, I didn't get it; that is, I didn't understand it. Or should I say, I didn't want to understand it. I didn't want to get it. At that time in my life my ego was doing one heck of a job on me. I thought I knew it all. I thought I had all the answers. I didn't like what she told me because it meant that I didn't know something. It also meant that I wouldn't be in control. My ego couldn't have that. So we did everything we could to discourage the idea. We came up with all kinds of logical reasons why it wouldn't work. The funny part about it was that no matter what we (my ego and I) did, it didn't work. All Ajanel did was surrender, allow and trust and no matter what I came up with, it held no weight. The irony of it all was that the harder I fought, the more it led me to surrender. It was like the saying, "If you can't beat 'em, join 'em." I eventually gave up and surrendered. She was having an amazing time and I was busy struggling and trying to prove my superiority. I was so afraid of losing control, that I became quite arrogant at times. In the end, I had no chance. The battle was over before it began. Any resistance proved futile.

As I began to read more of her writings, I told her that she needed to write a book and show this work to the world. So she did. It is called, <u>Surrender, Allow and Trust</u>. Much of what this chapter will discuss comes from her book. I highly recommend that you purchase a copy for yourself and get the full story. You can do so on www.surrenderallowandtrust.com and on my website, www.foreverfreetobe.com.

The basic tenet of surrender, allow and trust (SAT) is that you *surrender* in every moment, *allow* any possibility and *trust* the process completely and that the outcome will be a miracle. Then, simply, do what there is to do when it shows up to do.

Surrender, Allow and Trust – A Basic Outline

There are just a few things that will enable you to tap into your intuition and enable you to use it from now on, easily. I will list the main principles here briefly and then go over them in detail later on.

1. **Surrender** – Take yourself out of your own way. Take a load off. Turn on some relaxing music. Take a hot bath. Relax your body however you see fit. Find a comfortable place in the physical world where you can forget about the day. The best information comes when you are comfortable and at peace. Calm your mind. Be totally in the moment. Release your need to think, to try and figure everything out, to worry and to control everything. Your ego doesn't know what is best for you. Just let it all go. You can simply ask a question that you want an answer to and then move on to step two.

2. **Allow** – You can't force your intuition to work. Just be open. Visualize yourself as an open vessel being filled with all the information and support that you need. Many ideas will begin to come to you. Don't filter them out or rationalize them away. They would not come to you if you did not need them.

3. **Trust** – Trust yourself. You already have everything you need inside. Trust your gut. Trust the Universe. Trust your own inner wisdom. Trust the process completely and trust that the outcome will be a miracle. You will experience "Aha" moments as the answers seem to come from "out of the blue."

4. **Do** – Do give your intuition time to work. Do what there is to do when it shows up to do. Don't fight or resist it in any way. Do it in the moment you are given it to do. Don't hesitate or wait until later unless you are guided to do so. Sometimes the opportunity will only open for a very brief period of time.

So let's look at surrender, allow and trust in greater detail.

> ## "Following your intuition means
> ## thinking with your heart."
> ## – Ajanel

What is surrender?

Surrender is stopping the battle that is always going on inside of you, with yourself. As long as your ego is battling with itself, you can't surrender. It is the clearing of your mind and heart of everything that you have created in order for you to be able to hear the Universal messages that come to you. Surrendering is giving up the need to know how your life is going to look and allowing the Universe to determine the perfect outcome. When you switch from mind control to heart control, that is surrender. It is the feeling of falling in love without attachment. Surrender does not mean giving up. There is a great difference between surrender and giving up. Surrender allows you to take action. Giving up does not. Surrender is an active process. Giving up is passive. Surrender is power. Giving up is weak. Surrender involves a great deal of courage. Giving up is based in fear.

Your ego's job, once again, is to protect you from pain. When you struggle and resist and fight against the natural wisdom of your intuition, that makes your life very difficult. When you surrender, allow and trust, your life becomes much easier. Where the challenge comes in is that your ego wants to control everything and it does an absolutely amazing job of convincing you of its lies and making you believe that they are true. When you decide to take control back from your ego, through surrendering this moment, allowing the Universe's wisdom to speak to you, then trusting completely in the process and that the outcome will be a miracle, your life will take on a whole new meaning. When you SAT, you allow Infinite Intelligence to guide your every step, your every thought and to supply your every need, regardless of how you think it should be. In Ajanel's book, Infinite Intelligence says,

> When you surrender, you give up the need to know both the process and the outcome. You just have the faith to allow it. The whole thing. Process and outcome. Sometimes the process is for an entirely different outcome than the one you envision when you begin it. That is why you must surrender every moment, not just once. You may think you know the outcome, but you may not. Keep doing what there is to do and do not be attached to the outcome because the outcome may change.

What is allow?

Each of the four steps (Surrender, allow, trust and do) are equally important; that is, if you don't do any one of them, it automatically renders the other steps useless. However, there is a real, almost magical benefit to allowing all possibilities.

As far as surrender, allow and trust is concerned, when you allow any possibility, it truly means any possibility, including the one that comes right up and hits you in the face and makes you say, "Anything but that." Now let me be clear, you don't have to do all of the things that come to you, but one of them will just 'feel' right. You will just know that it is right for you. You may want to argue with it, but it will be pointless because you would only be fighting against yourself, your desires, your dreams and your intuition.

Allowing is NOT an act of creation. Allowing is openness for contribution. It begins with a willingness to listen and a sincere desire to change. Allowing is freedom from judgment. Allowing is being OK with everything exactly as it is and exactly as it is not. Please don't skip over that last sentence lightly. One of the reasons people struggle so much in their lives is that they resist change. They fight against what is; they push back when they are pushed. That's why resistance causes persistence. The more you fight against what is, yourself, or whatever, the more it will stay around. But when you allow any possibility, even the one that scares you to death, it automatically stops the resistance. For instance, if you are overweight, if you allow the possibility that it's OK in every way, shape and form, what will happen is that you will stop being consumed with food and diets and exercise, etc. You will stop putting all of that energy into the fight. Once you do that, you give yourself the freedom to change. In other words, by being OK to be heavy, you can be thin.

It is the same with your finances. If you are broke, instead of giving all of your energy to being broke and fighting debt, etc., simply allow the possibility that being broke is all right. Then it is much easier to focus on being wealthy. You see, whatever you give the most energy to, whether you're conscious of it or not, you will indeed keep creating over and over and over. So if you allow the possibility of being broke, instead of giving it energy through worry and doubt and fear, you are able to forget about it and start giving energy to what you really want...abundance.

So consider what you are resisting right now, allow the possibility that it is OK and allow all of the possibilities to come to you that will support you to resolve the situation most effectively.

In order for the things that you have *allowed* to come to fruition, you need to trust.

What is trust?

In the context of SAT, trust is very much like faith. It is knowing that something your intuition is telling you will happen even though there is no evidence or logical reason to believe that it will come true. In other words, you need to put yourself, your situation, your life completely in the hands of the unknown, fully believing that you will be cared for and that what you need will be provided...without exception. The trust I am talking about here is not like the trust you place in another. It is way beyond that and is far less risky. This type of trust will never steer you in the wrong direction and will never let you down. Trusting the process completely means going the distance until your desired goal has been achieved. It is not an active process in that there isn't anything that you need to do. Trusting, just like surrendering and allowing is a state of being. When you are someone who trusts, that will lead you to do what a trusting person does and that will enable you to have what a trusting person has. Trust takes commitment. Trust takes courage. Trust takes a strong conviction in your beliefs. If you don't trust the process completely, it won't work. If you don't trust that the outcome will be a miracle, you will block the process and you will not receive a miracle. Shakti Gawain says in her article entitled, *Art of Following Intuition,*

It's a matter of trusting that even when things are not going exactly the way you expected, there is a deeper perfection in the process. New forms of relationship, creativity, work, and home will come into being and they will reflect your growth and development.

For more understanding about how following your intuition can change your life, I suggest reading her book, <u>Living in the Light</u>.

What is, "Do what there is to do?"

Doing is the appropriate action you take after you have surrendered, allowed and trusted. You do what there is to do when it shows up to do. You do it as soon as you're guided. You follow the directions you've been given to the T. You don't second guess them. You don't doubt them. You act on them, knowing that what you do is going to allow you to have what you want. You may not understand them fully or see how the steps are going to work out, but that does not matter; you do them anyway. Anything less than this will sabotage the entire process.

If Intuition Is So Good, How Come We Don't All Listen To It?

There are many reasons for this.

- Some people don't even know that they have an intuition. They are completely unconscious.

- Some people think they know better and they second guess what their intuition is telling them. You can't know better because your intuition is based in a whole lot more than the tiny bit of information than your five senses allow you to experience. It is your 6th sense and it is clairsentient, clairvoyant, clairaudient.

- Some people fear that trusting their intuition will lead them to do things that are inappropriate or hurtful to others. Nothing could be further from the truth. Your intuition will always lead you in the direction of your highest and best good.

- Some people fear being wrong, being right, being rejected, being different. If they are wrong, they'll be judged. If they're right, they'll have to make some decisions that may be painful. If they are rejected, they'll be hurt. If they're different and they don't fit in anymore, they may lose friends.

- Some people fear change and being uncomfortable. When they are used to a certain way of living, they don't want that disrupted.

- Some people fear the negative judgments of others or that they may disappoint them. If you normally are a people pleaser and your intuition tells you to stop, the people you've been pleasing won't like it and won't like you. Even though it may not look like it, in the long run, everyone will be healthier and happier as a result.

- Some people don't believe in it. It's not rational or logical so they don't accept it.

- Some people distrust it. They believe that they have been misled by it in the past.

- Some people are afraid of how powerful it actually is. They see how easy their lives could be if they just "tuned in", but they are so used to struggle that they can't do it.

In closing, learning to follow and live by your intuition can sometimes feel like walking on a tightrope without a net. You may be afraid to move ahead and too scared to go back even though you're being pushed and pulled. Even though you can surrender to this moment and to the next and to the next, it won't matter. Even though you can allow that you will be totally safe, you still may not trust. Yet, if you did SAT, you would know beyond the shadow of a doubt that you would be safe.

You will be living your life from the safest place you could possibly live. You will be relying on infinite intelligence, not just your own, to guide you. You will be able to let go of a false sense of security that comes from trying to control everything that happens to you. At that point, change will become the norm. You'll enjoy the perfection of what not controlling everything allows and you'll begin to enjoy the process. Stepping out of your comfort zone will be more comfortable than living in it. You'll start to feel alive, passionate, free and you'll have a great deal more energy. Your confidence will soar as you recognize that as you follow your inner wisdom and your inner truth, it will take you to places and have you experience wonders that you've never even dreamed of...and then some! It is like opening a gift. You don't know what is inside until you open it. And when you do, the joy and abundance you will feel will far surpass all of your expectations.

Transformational Questions

1. How do you define intuition for yourself?

   _____

   _____

2. Do you believe that following your intuition will support you in your life or business or both? Yes or No? _____ Why or why not?

   _____

   _____

3. Do you trust your gut (follow your intuition) all the time? Yes or No?

   _____

4. If your answer is no, please explain why? _____

   _____

   _____

5. Write down a situation in which against all reasoning, you followed your intuition and it worked out better than you could have ever planned.

_____

_____

_____

6. What happened as a result?

_____

_____

_____

7. Describe a situation in which your gut was screaming at you to do something and you didn't listen to it.

_____

_____

8. What happened as a result?

_____

_____

9. Do you think that if you fully trust your intuition, it won't work? Yes or No? _____ Please explain your answer.

_____

_____

_____

10. Do you believe the Universe will give you whatever you ask for? Yes or No? _____ Please explain.

_____

_____

11. If your answer is yes, then what stops you from having all that you desire?

_____

_____

12. **If your answer is no, then do you have a better way of doing things than the Universe? Yes or No? _____ Please explain.**

_____

_____

13. **Explain how you're going to use your intuition differently now.**

_____

_____

_____

Summary Of Key Ideas And Important Points

1. Don't be afraid of your intuition.
2. Your intuition will never lead you astray.
3. Your intuition is the Universe talking to you.
4. You are not smarter than your intuition. You can't outthink it.
5. There is no shortcut to getting around what it tells you. What it tells you IS the shortcut.
6. Surrendering, allowing and trusting enables you to benefit most from your intuition.
7. You must surrender, allow and trust, then do. If you leave any one out, it won't work.
8. Your ego is about survival. Your intuition is about freedom.
9. Your intuition is always there, guiding you. Just tune in by getting out of your head.
10. You build the intuition muscle just like any other muscle, over time and with use.

CHAPTER 7

LOVE REALLY IS ALL THERE IS

"Love is the emblem of eternity: it confounds
all notion of time: effaces all memory of a
beginning, all fear of an end." – Germaine De Stael

My Life Without Love...A Very Personal Journey

What I am about to share are some of the most personal experiences, thoughts and feelings that I have experienced in my life, or shared with the public for that matter. I decided to be even more personal in this chapter than in the other ones because that is what love would do. Love dictates that I share my deepest self with you so that you know that it's safe to let that part out of you and transform your relationship to it. The journey from where you are now, to living as love is one of the most amazing experiences you can go through. It certainly has been that way for me. With love, anything is possible. Without it, there is emptiness, loneliness, fear and pain. And it is in those places that I have spent most of my life.

When it came to love, I was a complete novice. I didn't know anything. I had all the ideas about love, all the concepts rolling around in my brain, but there was no connection to my heart. My head and my heart were about as disconnected and as distant as they could be. I truly did not want to feel anything. I didn't want anyone to get close to me. I didn't want to let anyone in. I had been hurt too many times and I wasn't about to let it happen again. I was lonely. I was afraid. I wasn't comfortable in my own skin. I didn't feel good about who I was. I felt like I didn't belong. I felt like a misfit who didn't even fit in with the misfits. I didn't love myself, nor did I even entertain the idea. In my life, I was just going through the motions, existing, with little else. Everyday was filled with the pain of loneliness, the solitude of separation and a desperate desire for connection, for acceptance…for love. On the very few occasions when it did come, I didn't know what to do with it, so I pushed it away. I ruined all of my relationships. I picked women to date who I could fix just so they would need me. I had a desperate need to be needed. At least that way I was wanted for a short while. But those relationships never lasted long. They couldn't. There was nothing to them. They were based on illusions…just like my life.

I wouldn't let good things happen to me because I wasn't worthy of them. I believed I was unnecessary and therefore nothing good should, could or would come my way. I had a strong shield around my whole body to protect me from the 'evils' of love. Love was too painful, too all consuming. It left me vulnerable, weak and open to more pain. I would do anything not to feel that pain, that despair. I felt unwanted and unneeded. Being with that was unbearable, so I shut down and I turned my pain into anger.

Anger became my default emotion. I, like most men, was taught to repress every emotion, with the exception of anger and I did it well. Yet I only selectively showed my anger to certain people. I couldn't show it to the general public because then I would alienate even more people. I just took it out on the ones I loved the most. I was a walking bag of anger. Because I couldn't show it during the day, I would grind my teeth in my sleep. I would sometimes wake up with my teeth loose because I clamped down on them so hard for so long each night. My dentist even commented on them one day. That was a big wake-up call. So I started to ask myself, what I was so angry about. There was no apparent reason. There was just an ever-present rage inside and I couldn't figure out what was causing it. The truth was, as I looked back on it, I don't think I wanted to know why I was angry. The anger served me. It protected me…at least that's what I thought. Of course, the exact opposite was true.

When it came to my business, I cared about people more than they cared about themselves. I was a chameleon, being whatever people wanted. What I was doing was trying to prove to myself and everyone around me that I was a good person and that I had only the best intentions. In effect, I made my whole life about everyone else to prove something that didn't need proving. I didn't need to prove anything to anyone. All of that always resulted in pain and upset and sadness, but I did it over and over and over. I even went so far as to take responsibility for people and their growth. Of course, that's not possible. It always resulted in me being hurt, dejected and at a loss.

I also became a know-it-all. I closed my mind to a great deal of things and I would not let people contribute to me. I was extremely arrogant at times. I was very overbearing when I thought I was just deeply caring about people and trying to help them.

But all of that was about me when all the while, I thought what I was doing was for everyone else. I was doing all of this in a desperate attempt to be loved. I worked so hard at it that it had the opposite effect. Suffice it to say that my life was full of confusion, doubt, fear and pain. But please don't get me wrong. I wasn't crazy. I wasn't suicidal. I wasn't psychotic. I never took drugs, prescription or otherwise. I never used alcohol to escape either. I didn't need them and I didn't want them.

The Day My Anger Began To Turn Around

I went to a workshop in 1997 to help me to safely transform my anger. It was a cathartic experience to say the least. We were directed to hit a heavy bag with whatever objects of destruction that were used on us when we were children. I saw men beat that bag with belts, sticks, bats and various other things. I watched them beat that bag with everything they had. I watched them do this while I cowered in the corner, sobbing, saying, "That's not me. I don't have any anger." I got so afraid that I started to hyperventilate. Yet I was still in denial that I was angry. In fact, I didn't even want to admit that I had any anger at all. I then developed tetany. It is a condition that temporarily locks your body up and you can't move. I was paralyzed by my anger. The facilitator walked up to me and said, "Look what this is doing to you. Do you want it to control you for the rest of your life or do you want to get rid of it now?" I wanted it gone, but I was too afraid. By this time, I could barely open my mouth because of the tetany. My fingers were clenched so tight, you couldn't pry them apart if you tried. The facilitator gave me one final chance to go to the heavy bag. I fearfully agreed. It took a minute or so to try and work the bat into my fingers. I went up to that bag, looked at it and felt sorry for it for what I was about to do to it.

The anger was my survival. When that was gone, what would be left? It didn't matter. I had to hit the bag. So, I did. The first shot was such a release. I don't even know how the bag stayed attached. I had been so afraid to show my anger for fear that people would avoid me even more. But I was still alive.

The next shot was harder. The next, even harder. I continued with each passing shot to dump the poison out of me. I ran through all the visions in my head of all the abuses, hurts, pains and traumas I endured. I made that bag pay for what had happened to me. I wanted to split that bag into a thousand pieces and then really do some damage to it. The damn thing wouldn't break. That pissed me off even more. Needless to say, I wore out before it did. After five minutes, I had nothing left. When I was done, I collapsed. I couldn't even move for about forty-five minutes. I let years of anger go in just a few minutes. I was drained, but I was liberated. For the first time in years, I wasn't mad anymore. When I stopped running from my anger, it stopped running me.

> "Love is an eternally blooming flower and you
> are the garden that gives it life."
> – Darshan Shanti.

How Love Saved My Life

When my anger was gone, what naturally was left was the real me. That real me, just like your real you is made of love. But love was foreign to me. I didn't understand it and I didn't know how to access it. It was one thing to be free from my anger. It was quite another to begin to live as love. Well it came to me from a place I least expected it to come from. I was leading a group of people in a weekly get together to share ideas with one another to help our businesses grow. Week after week I would beg and plead with the people and try to convince them that they could do anything, that they really could be happy and could live the lives they want and truly attain success. It was a fight every week. I couldn't understand why they didn't 'get it'. No matter what I did, all my efforts were in vain. Yet somewhere in me I knew all of this was about me.

The person I was talking to about all of those things was really me. I was begging and pleading with myself to start to love myself, not just everyone else. They couldn't get it because I didn't get it. Although I didn't know it at the time, I needed them to help me to see myself. As long as I kept working on them, I didn't have to work on myself. I was trying to be successful and live vicariously through them. I mistakenly thought that if I helped enough people get what they wanted, then I would get what I want. I now know that's not true.

What is true is that if I help enough people get what they want, while loving myself, believing in myself and in what I do and I take the appropriate action, then I will get what I want.

During one of my 'coaching' talks, one of the men in the group said to me, "You keep telling us how great we are, well, how great are you?" It was like a wave of truth came up and barreled in to me and then consumed me like a tsunami. There was nowhere to go. There was nothing to do. There was no denying it. I broke down and sobbed and sobbed and sobbed. I was exposed to myself and to everyone in that room. That was my most vulnerable moment. I remember saying to him, "You weren't supposed to get through." Can you imagine that? As hard as my life was, I didn't want to change. I somehow thought that living the way I was living was less painful. My denial was so deep, so all consuming and so relentlessly painful and yet, I wouldn't let it go. I couldn't let it go for fear that if I lost my illusion of reality, I would have nothing. You can go back and read *The Grand Irony of Life* once more if you would like a further explanation of why I was hanging on.

As you may imagine, that started a chain of events that will continue for the rest of my life. After all the crying, in that moment, I was a new man. In that moment, my triangle no longer had power over me. In that moment, I was just me. Life didn't look the same. I didn't feel the same. I began to get excited. I was reborn. For the first time I felt whole, complete and OK to be who I was. I didn't have to apologize for being me anymore.

The effectiveness of the work I was doing with people in my seminars went through the roof. They were getting the results that used to take weeks in just a few hours. Business became easier and it came to me easier. People just started saying yes all the time. Now was it perfect? No. Did I live happily ever after? No. But what I did do was regain my health, greatly increase my wealth, attract many new friends and I enhanced my romantic relationship with Ajanel. She is the most incredible example of unconditional love and acceptance that I have ever seen. I owe my life to her. Without her patience, wisdom, tenderness, acceptance, love and so many, many, many little things that she does for me, I am not sure where my life would be now or if I even would have still been here. She is truly my guardian angel, my light, my guide and my greatest blessing. Ajanel. I love you! And thanks to you, I know what that means now. Thank you for giving me the gift of me through the mirror of you. Thank you for helping me to find my heart that you knew was always in there somewhere. Thank you for standing by me and never giving up until I became who you knew I was all along. I look forward to a beautiful life together.

What Is Love? Let's Look At It Closely

That's one heck of a question to answer. I mean, how do you define the indefinable? How do you measure the immeasurable? How do you describe the indescribable? How do you limit the unlimited and put boundaries on the infinite?

Most everything you have ever been taught about love is way off base. Love has been taught as an idea, an unrealizable fantasy, an illusion, a fairy tale, a place to get to. Believing that does more harm than good. Just think of the lie at the end of so many children's books, "And they lived happily ever after." What a joke. Who do you know that actually lives happily ever after? Yet it implants the ideas in the brains of so many children that finding a relationship will bring eternal happiness. How many relationships have failed because of that? The second your partner doesn't bring you the ever-present bliss you think she's supposed to bring you, out the door she goes. And it's on to the next one. The second he leaves his socks on the floor, out he goes. If we live that fantasy, we're in for a whole lot of problems. If we can't find that eternal happiness in a partner, we may look for it in alcohol, drugs, sex, food, etc.

According to Abraham Maslow and his hierarchy of needs, the second from the bottom is safety. If in your childhood experiences, you felt unsafe, unloved, unwanted or unaccepted and if your parents were negative, uncaring or emotionally absent, then you will probably be that way in relationships as an adult. The problem is that causes you to act as a deprived, wounded, isolated child even if you're fifty-years old. It causes you to go looking everywhere you can to fill your need to be accepted. That is, to get the love that you never felt you got when you were a child. That causes all relationships to fail. And since most of us have been taught to look outside of ourselves for love, that sets us up to fail as well. So if we don't love ourselves on the inside, we'll never be able to quench our thirst for it on the outside. The love that we are all looking for is an illusion which causes us to not be able to see or feel the love that is always present.

In addition, many of us fear love. We fear how powerful it is. We fear it because we don't understand it. We try to protect ourselves from it. In order to stop fearing it, you have to rethink what you have been taught about love. You have to define what love means to you. Then you must take a very deep look at yourself. Every single thing that you don't like about yourself or your life, you must let go. Forgive what you can forgive and forget the rest. Holding on to any negative belief about yourself only serves to suck the life energy out of you.

Once you forgive, you don't have to work at filling the unmet needs of your childhood.

C.S. Lewis On Love

Love anything and your heart will be wrung and possibly broken. If you want to make sure of keeping it intact, you must give it to no one, not even an animal. Wrap it carefully round with hobbies and little luxuries; avoid all entanglements. Lock it up safe in the casket or coffin of your selfishness. But in that casket, safe, dark, motionless, airless, it will change. It will not be broken; it will become unbreakable, impenetrable and irredeemable. To love is to be vulnerable.

Where We Learn About "Love"

All forms of media (TV, movies, magazines, music, ads, billboards, romance novels, adult videos and adult magazines, children's books, friends, school, family, church, etc.

They Lead Us To Believe That Love Is

Romance, infatuation, negative, conditional, selfish, controlling, confusing, fearful, shameful, hurtful, sex, painful, unsafe, magical, manipulative, obligatory, sacrificial, quick, always electrifying

The Negative Effects Of That Way Of Believing Are

Victimization, distrust, manipulation, guilt, pain, separation/alone, being turned off, being resigned, being cynical, feeling used, feeling wronged, feeling unfulfilled, feeling empty, self-doubtful, feeling ashamed, codependence, feeling cheated and in the end, we feel that love is a lie

Yet True Love Is

Healthy, non-judgmental, open, boundless, free, beautiful, unattached, easy, sensitive, giving, compassionate, positive, understanding, creative, unconditional, the energy of life and living, dynamic, alive and growing.

So, take a look in your own life and see if my story applies to you in any area.

See where you're attached to certain outcomes that are based in what you want rather than what's best for the situation. See where you try to control someone or some situation. See where you may know-it-all and not allow people's love or support. See where your life is not working the way you want and then ask for help. It will come.

Love – A Quantum Physics Perspective

Scientists tell us that the smallest substances on earth (atoms) are mostly space – about 99.99%. And since everything is made of atoms, then the entire Universe is mostly 'empty.' To me, love is the space between that emptiness. Love is the emptiness of the emptiness. Outside of that emptiness, everything else exists (1/100 of 1 percent). Love is the only thing that matters. Love is matter. It can't be created or destroyed. Love just is.

Another way of looking at it is that love is the glue that holds the Universe together. To me, love is pure energy. It has no beginning and no end, yet it is the beginning and the end and all points in between. Were it not for this force, we would not be here. Some people decide to call that force, God. I yield to Shakespeare at this point. Juliet Capulet said to Romeo Montague, "What's in a name? That which we call a rose by any other name would smell as sweet."

From a quantum physics perspective, love can be seen as the field of all possibilities. The point is that love really is everything, in everyone and is everywhere all the time. It's like energy. It was in the beginning, is now and always shall be. If that's the case, then you are love. Regardless of what you've thought about yourself or continue to think, you are love for you could not be anything else. The problem is that most people don't realize that and therefore don't live that way. I wrote a poem that sums love up for me.

LOVE

God created love so that we could be
Closer to understanding God's Universality
God is love, the omniscient totality
Therefore love is the only reality.

The Human Affliction... We Don't Believe In Or Love Ourselves Unconditionally

The foundation of a great life, great relationships, great friends, great happiness, great joy, and great satisfaction is directly related to how much we love ourselves. And the exact opposite is true as well. You just read what my life was like without it. Now if we look around, it's quite easy to see how few people understand this.

Take Owen Wilson for example. He tried to kill himself by slitting his wrists and taking a bunch of pills. What would cause a good looking, wealthy, famous actor to want to end his life? He could have anything he wanted. He could have had any relationship. He could have gone anywhere, done anything and experienced whatever he wanted. Yet he tried to kill himself instead. Does that seem logical to you? It is if you can begin to imagine what kind of pain he was in. When someone gets to such a low point that death is far less painful than living even one more day, there's a serious problem because the pain is so much and so deep that it's just not worth it to continue.

Do you really think that if Owen loved himself, valued himself, honored, respected, believed, cherished and liked himself that he would have tried to kill himself? Of course he wouldn't have. And, Ana Nicole Smith, John Belushi, River Phoenix, Chris Farley and a whole host of other famous people would not have been successful at taking their own lives either. And it would not have mattered how much pain they were in.

The World's Love Project

It is my contention that if everyone knew their pricelessness and was *in love* with themselves, we wouldn't have the problems we currently are facing all over the globe. Wars would not exist because they couldn't. Neither would crimes, murders, suicides, and any other acts of hatred. I have decided that I no longer want to be part of the problem and I want to be part of the solution. I have complained for years about what is happening in this world and felt powerless to have any kind of impact. That no longer holds true for me anymore because of the internet. Through the power of the internet, a huge difference can be made. I am starting a global project called, 'The World's Love Project' to help shift the consciousness of the people on this planet to love and connection. Together, we can change the world.

The vision is: A World United In Love

The mission is: To share the message of love with as many people as possible through every medium possible all over the world.

I envision an international day of love, globally recognized and practiced. I envision at least 1 billion people simultaneously sending love all over the world. No doubt, that will shift the consciousness of anger and violence and war and separation to one of peace, kindness and connection.

If this inspires you and you would like to be a part of it, please visit,

www.theworldsloveproject.org and see what part you can play.

What Rocky Balboa Taught Us About Love

One of the best lines from Rocky III was when Rocky told Adrian that he was scared for the first time in his life to fight. He had given up. He had lost his edge. He was, for all intents and purposes, done. Adrian was pressing him for the truth. That's when Rocky said, "Nothing is real if you don't believe in who you are."

Take a moment to really consider how powerful that statement is.

"Nothing is real if you don't believe in who you are."

Rocky told Adrian that in his early days he didn't care about himself or his life, so he would fight anyone because it didn't matter what happened to him. But then he began to care about himself, his family and all the good things he had. He didn't want to lose them. All of a sudden, he mattered. His life mattered. Then his entire perspective changed.

It is the same for you. If you don't believe in yourself, or as I would say, if you don't love yourself, what do you have? Let me be clear about what I mean when I say, LOVE YOURSELF. I don't just mean that you're OK with who you are. I mean that you love yourself as much as you love your family or your children or your spouse or the people in your life that you would do anything for because you love them so much.

When you love yourself on that level, your self-esteem skyrockets, your productivity increases greatly, your relationships change for the better and your dreams become possible because your fear fades away. You make more money, experience true joy and stress doesn't affect you the same way. The benefits are truly limitless.

All the riches in the world can't make up for an empty heart. Neither will all the food, all the drugs, all the gambling, all the sex, all the relationships or all the booze. Just look at the lives of Brittany Spears, Paris Hilton, Michael Jackson, Ozzy, Courtney Love, Whitney Houston, Amy Winehouse, Robert Downey Jr., Nicole Ritchie, etc. The point is that YOU CAN NEVER GET ENOUGH OF WHAT YOU DON'T ALREADY HAVE.

"Love alone is capable of uniting living beings in such a way as to complete and fulfill them, for it alone takes them and joins them by what is deepest in themselves."
– Pierre Teilhard de Chardin

The Wizard of Oz And You

In reality, you are a champion and you already have the heart of a champion. You must realize that in order for it to take affect.

In The Wizard of Oz, the Wizard gave the tin man a testimonial (the heart shaped clock) to symbolize that which he already had, but didn't think he did. He gave the lion a medal to symbolize the courage he had all along. And he gave the brain of the bunch a diploma. Why did he give them such trivial things? Because he couldn't give to them what they already had. As the rock group America sings, "No Oz never did give nothing to the Tin Man that he didn't, didn't already have."

But he had nothing in his little bag of tricks for Dorothy because she too had everything she needed within her all of the time. The Good Witch told Dorothy that she had the power to go back to Kansas anytime she wanted to. When the witch was asked why she never told Dorothy, she said, "Because she wouldn't have believed me. She had to learn it for herself." Dorothy learned a very valuable lesson. It was that if she ever went searching for her heart's desire again, she didn't need to go searching any further than her own backyard because if it wasn't there, she never really lost it to begin with. She also had to discover that for herself before she could go home.

The point is that you too don't have to go looking anywhere for love. It's in you right now. It has the power to take you anywhere you want to go. It has the power to make your life anything you want it to be. It has the power to heal the world. You have that power too and you can do it best by loving yourself and then sharing that love with anyone and everyone.

Take a look at your life and what you are doing that is not serving you and then consider the following scenarios. If any of them apply to you, then you have a decision to make. You can continue going down the same path, doing the same things, getting the same results, all the while being frustrated or you can simply decide to do what love would do and you'll have a life that love brings.

Do any of the following apply to you?

Are you working yourself to death?
Are you in a career you don't like?
Are you in a relationship that has long outgrown its purpose?
Are you not doing what you really want to do with your life?
Have you put your dreams on permanent hold?
Do you sacrifice yourself for others over and over?
Are you eating poorly (too much, not enough, unhealthy)?
Are you not exercising?
Are you smoking?
Are you drinking too much?
Are you...fill in the blank?

Then ask yourself what unmet needs you may have that you're trying to fill? When you find some, go to the root cause and deal with them. Don't just put band aids on it. True champions don't mask their problems; they deal with them. Answering the following questions will help you to do just that.

Transformational Questions

1. How do you personally define love?

   _____

   _____

2. How do you personally define unconditional love?

   _____

   _____

3. Do you love yourself as much, more or less than your spouse, your children, your friends, etc.? Yes or No? _____ Explain.

   _____

   _____

4. Do you believe you deserve all the love and good things life has to offer? Yes or No? _____

5. If not, why not?

   _____

   _____

6. Do you have a fear of being loved (letting people love you)? Yes or No? _____ Explain.

   _____

   _____

7. Do you withhold love from yourself or others? Yes or No? _____

8. If you do, what's the reason?

   _____

   _____

9. Do you believe that you are worthy of being loved?

   _____

   _____

10. Are you uncomfortable with the subject of love? Yes or No? _____

11. **If so, why?** _____

12. **What is your most painful memory regarding love?** It doesn't matter if it came from your childhood or your adulthood or any point in between.

   _____

   _____

   _____

13. **What is your most pleasureful memory regarding love?** Once again, it doesn't matter if it came from your childhood or your adulthood or a point in between.

   _____

   _____

14. **Where did you learn what love is?**

   _____

   _____

15. **Who were your role models that taught you about love and what was their relationship like?**

   _____

   _____

16. **What negative associations or fears do you have with love and as a result, it stops you from loving or allowing yourself to be loved?** When you discover these negative associations, they instantly will be invalidated. As an adult, you won't need them anymore.

   _____

   _____

17. **What positive associations do you have with love?** You should start focusing on these.

   _____

   _____

18. **How do you feel when you think about love?**

   _____

   _____

19. Are there any barriers (thoughts, feelings, beliefs) that are still pre-
venting you from loving yourself unconditionally from now on? If
there are, list them here.

_____

_____

20. If there are barriers, what are you going to do so that they don't stop
you anymore?

_____

_____

To close this most beautiful chapter, I'll leave you with another poem I
wrote. Use it as a guide in times of need.

WHAT WOULD LOVE DO?

What would love have you do?
That's the only thing to listen to
When you're in doubt, pain or fear
And you're just not sure, just not clear

And you're wondering which move to make
Which direction to go, which step to take
Just put yourself in love's place and ask
What would love do with this task?

Love lets go where fear holds tight
Love is never about being right
And love leaves people completely free
To be who they are, not who we want them to be

'Cause love will never lead you astray
Love could never be that way
For love is FREEDOM without limitation
A boundlessly open, unattached sensation

"Love, like truth and beauty, is concrete. Love is not fundamentally a sweet feeling; not, at heart, a matter of sentiment, attachment, or being "drawn toward." Love is active, effective, a matter of making reciprocal and mutually beneficial relation with one's friends and enemies."
– Carter Heyward

May you look into your soul everyday and tell it, "I Love You." And may it look back to you and tell you the same thing.

Summary Of Key Ideas And Important Points

1. Love is all there is.
2. Love doesn't need to explain itself.
3. Love doesn't judge.
4. Love yourself first.
5. You are love and love is you.
6. Love is not something to be afraid of.
7. Love is the life force of this planet.
9. You are a cell in the body of love.
10. If you don't go within yourself to find love, you will go without.

CHAPTER 8

THE ART OF BALANCE

"A well-developed sense of humor is the
pole that adds balance to your steps as you
walk the tightrope of life." – William Arthur Ward

We live in a crazy world now. We are bombarded each day with more information, more choices, more opportunities, more TV channels, more restaurants, more perfumes (there are over 1000) more obligations, more responsibilities, more ways to be gotten a hold of, etc., etc. Yet we seem to have less time to manage it all. Of course, we still all have the same twenty-four hours, it's just how those hours are being used up by so many different things that we deem important. That's where the art of balance comes in.

What this chapter aims to help you do is to put your entire life into perspective. You'll look at the six major life areas and you'll see what's out of balance and you'll then learn how you can deal with each of them in a more effective way.

Take a look at the chart on the next page. There are six different major life areas. In the center is the number 0 and on the outside is a number 10. Go through each of the sections and rate yourself on a scale of 1 to 10. Then draw a curved line in each segment that approximates where you have rated yourself. When you're done, you should have a balance pie chart that doesn't look very balanced at all. Some areas will be a 2 and some will be a 6 and some will be an 8. The point is, your wheel won't spin too well if it is out of balance like that. This chart will give you an idea of which area(s) of your life needs the most attention. Now, if everything is a 2 and so the wheel is balanced, that still doesn't work because you want all of the sections to be rated much higher.

In addition, these labels on this chart can be anything you want them to be. These six life areas could be all different on your chart. Your chart could have more than six. It could include religion/spirituality. It could include anything you want it to include. It's your life. Balance it however you see fit.

HOW BALANCED IS YOUR LIFE?

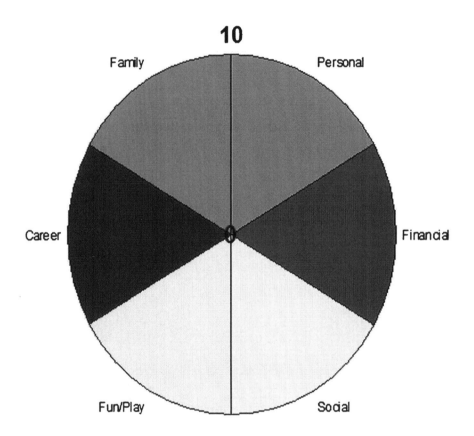

Now answer the following questions to further put your life balance picture together.

1. How do you define balance?

   _____

   _____

2. Is your life out of balance now? Yes or No? _____

3. If it is out of balance, in what areas is it out?

   _____

   _____

   _____

4. Is that a recurring pattern? In other words, do those areas seem to be out of balance regularly? Yes or No? _____

5. If your answer is yes, what do you think the reason is?

   _____

   _____

6. Do you believe it's possible to have perfect balance all the time? Yes or No? _____

7. When things get out of balance in your life, how does that make you feel? Be specific.

   _____

   _____

8. When things get out of balance in your life, what happens to your productivity?

   _____

   _____

9. Describe what your life looks like when things get way out of balance. For example, are you going from place to place always in a mad rush?

Are you running all the time but never getting anywhere? Do you never have enough time to get everything done?

_____

_____

_____

10. **What does that cost you emotionally, mentally, physically?** Once again, be specific. The reason is that you really need to feel all of your emotions. Don't' be afraid of your anger or your tears. Let them come out. Just be with them.

_____

_____

_____

_____

Some General Areas To Look At To See What's Out Of Balance

You know if you're out of balance just by looking at some general life areas and asking yourself some basic questions like:

Do I have time for myself and the things I want to do? Do I have time for fun in my life? Am I overweight, underweight, tired more often than I used to be, stressed constantly, regularly feeling sick or run down, anxious, constantly worried, forgetful or on the edge?

You get the idea. If you answered yes to many of them, your life is way out of balance. The good news is that once you slow down enough to see it, you can then put a plan in place to begin to bring more balance to your life. Just keep asking yourself the following questions.

Am I doing anything now that is unnecessarily adding stress and problems and overwhelm to my life? Yes or No? _____

If I am doing things that are adding stress, problems and overwhelm to my life, what are they?

_____

_____

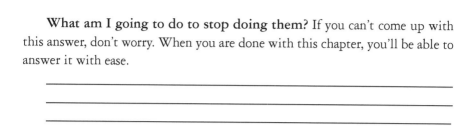

What am I going to do to stop doing them? If you can't come up with this answer, don't worry. When you are done with this chapter, you'll be able to answer it with ease.

Now that you have a general picture of how balanced or imbalanced your life is, it will put the rest of this chapter in perspective and will give you a better sense of how best to proceed.

The Four Key Steps Of Balance

I have looked long and hard at how to balance life and work as mine has been out of balance for so long. Usually my life was way too much work and not enough fun, play, relaxation. I was (and still am) in many aspects a workaholic. That's partly due to the fact that I absolutely love what I do. I eat, sleep and breathe personal development. It brings me the most joy and excitement to be on stage in front of 1000's of people. It is where I belong.

Now, you too may be a workaholic and love what you do or you may be out of balance because you have a large family and so it's not a problem for you. What this chapter aims to do is help you to bring balance back to the areas you want to bring balance to.

There are dozens and dozens of things that you can do to bring balance to your life, but what I wanted to do is to distill all of those things down into what I believe are the most important things that will give you a foundation on which you can build the rest of your life upon. You will never achieve perfect balance, nor would you want to. That would be called boredom. Then you would have to create some drama in your life and make things out of balance again because you would be too bored otherwise. So here are the four steps.

1 – Know that balance all begins with you (you're the foundation)
2 – Know your values (the traits that are the most important to you)

3 – Know your top three to five priorities (the activities, people, etc that are the most important and systematically get rid of all the time wasters)

4 – Know your boundaries (set them and stick to them)

So let's take each one of them separately and go to work on it.

Know That It All Begins With You... Just Like Everything Else

By far, the most important thing when it comes to creating balance in your life is that without a doubt, you are the most important priority in your life. Don't apologize for that. You are the center of everything. You are the focal point. Without you, there is nothing. Therefore everything in your world revolves around you. As I like to say, "This is it. That's it. You're it. There's nothing more to it." That does not mean that the world or anyone in it owes you anything. It just means that without you, there is nothing. Your life will quickly fall into shambles if you don't live that way. As I have said many, many times in this book, value, honor, cherish, respect and love yourself first, then focus on everyone and everything else that you want to.

There is a journey that you will be making as you go through this process. It is the journey from being selfish to self-centered to selfless. In chapter three, I shared my definitions of the first two. I'll repeat them here to refresh your memory. And I'll share what the third one is. Being selfish is a fear based way to live. To me, it's rooted in survival. It's a, 'there's not enough' mentality. The selfish person doesn't want to share and protects everything he has. Being self-centered is a much healthier perspective. The self-centered person takes care of himself first because he knows he must or he can't be there for others. He makes himself his number one priority and he has no regrets or qualms about that.

Being selfless, on the other hand, is like being a candle light that freely goes everywhere and lights every candle that wants to be lit because it knows it will always be lit no matter what. Selfless people have little concern for themselves because they have all their needs met already.

When and if you reach the selfless stage is not that important. What's important is that you are on the journey and you're growing towards that space.

Now take a look at each of the areas in your balance pie chart that you would like to work on. For the purposes of making it easier on you, just pick one that you really feel is out of sync. As you go through the rest of the exercises in this chapter, apply what you learn to that area.

Know Your Values

Your values are the most important things to you and literally dictate what you do and don't do. You have to be your number one value. For example, if you value comfort and safety more than risk and adventure, you'll have a completely different life. Your values help you set your boundaries. They help you prioritize. They help you to say, "NO." Your values in essence are your guidance system. They steer you in the right direction and together with your feelings, they let you know when you are on or off course. As Dr. John DMartini says, "What you value you perceive to be missing in your life. Naturally that creates a void and we don't like voids so we seek to fill them up." In other words, what you value, you move toward. And what you don't value, you move away from.

So many of the problems people have in their lives are due to the fact that they are living out the value systems that their parents gave them, their religious upbringing gave them, their teachers, friends, coworkers gave them. They have never stopped to reconsider them and/or consider what is important to them now. In other words, most of the building you have built and called *your life* has been built with other people's stuff.

Well, that's all about to change right now.

The following series of exercises will help you to really clarify your values. Since the following charts are rather small, I have a special place on my website that you can visit to download each of these full size charts. Simply go to **www.the24hourchampion.com** and click on the Templates tab, then click on any of the following 'Possible Values', 'Values Clarification', 'Values Prioritization', 'Integrity Circle', 'Outegrity Circle'.

Take a look at the following chart and in each column there are fifteen values, or as I like to call them, states of being, to choose from. There are also spaces at the end of each column that are blank. They are there for you to write in your own values to add to the ones I have listed. There are many, many 1000's of words I could have picked to make up this chart, so I am sure that you can think of some that are important to you that aren't listed. One way to do that is to write down a list of ten of the people you admire most in the world and list at least three to five character traits about each of them that you like. Those traits that you write down are what's important to you and you either have them in your life now or you want them. In any case, they are what you value.

What you need to do now is go through the chart and put a little number one next to each of the values that you like. You'll be going through the chart twice, once now and once in a little while. That's the reason for the number one. Between all the values listed in the chart and all the ones you write in, make sure you have at least thirty. I don't care if you have all seventy-five checked and have written in seventy-five of your own. Just put that little number one next to each of the values you like.

Some Possible Values To Choose From

Vision	Unstoppable	Thinking	Self-Expression	Courage
Love	Fun	Health	Purpose	Inspiration
Respect	Truth	Trust	Healing	Release
Myself	Independence	Commitment	Balance	Imagination
Humor	Leadership	Conscious	Strength	Motivation
Intimacy	Prosperity	Compassion	Affection	Wisdom
Giving	A job well done	Willingness	Honesty	Power
Receiving	Being my word	Magic	Communication	Openness
Full On Living	Peace/Harmony	Listening	Understanding	Determination
Making a Difference	Personal Growth and Development	Example of good	God/Spirituality/ Faith	Full Self-Acceptance
Confidence	Competence	Wholeness	Forgiveness	Completeness
Passion	Caring	Learning	Actualization	Awareness
Adventure	Risk	Laughter	Joy	Play
Creativity	Go Getter	Fitness	Transformation	Charisma
Honor	Responsibility	Surrender	Gratitude	Intuition

OK, now comes the fun part. It can also be quite challenging because what you are going to do now is start to clarify and prioritize which of those are the most important to you.

On the following page is a chart that has seven columns. The first column is labeled, TOP thirty. In that column, you need to narrow the values you selected down to thirty. So if you picked fifty of them from my list and wrote in twenty of your own, what you now will do is narrow that list of seventy, down into thirty.

What most people do is start to look at each one and say to themselves something like, "Well this one is similar to this, so I'll delete it." Or, "These few can be under the umbrella of this one, so I can eliminate them."

Take your time with this. Your values are the foundation of the new life you're creating. You're consciously creating who you are. If you build a building on a poorly made foundation, it will surely crumble. You are building your life building and you need it to be strong and be able to last a long, long time. So don't rush through this exercise. It is designed to force you to think about what you really believe to be important for you in your life. It is designed for you to keep narrowing down your values so that you can see what your number one, most important value is. Go ahead and write in the top 30 now. Then follow the directions on the next page.

TOP 30	TOP 20	TOP 15	TOP 10	TOP 5	TOP 3	TOP 1

Values Clarification

Now, which 10 values of those 30 that you just wrote can you live without? In the top 20 column, simply transfer the 20 values that are the most important from the top 30 column. Do the same thing with the top 15 column. Once again, which 5 of the top 20 can you live without and that will give you the top 15. Go on down the line doing the same thing until you reach your top 1. Please do not write in your top 1 before you get there through the process I just described. You may think that you know what it is now, but after you go through the exercise, it will more than likely change. In fact, out of all the times I have given this out to my live audiences, there have only been a handful of times in which the person wrote in his #1 value first and it remained the same.

Good luck with this. Again, take your time to build a rock solid life foundation.

Congratulations! I am sure that was a tough process. It is for everyone. If you haven't done it yet, please go back and do it. You will be doing yourself an amazing disservice if you don't.

In any event, were you surprised by anything you learned? If so, what was it? Jot a note or two about it here.

_____

_____

_____

Was your number one value different than you thought it was? Yes or No? What does that tell you about yourself and what's important to you?

_____

_____

_____

When you are first forming your values, they will rapidly change because you will be rapidly growing. What was important to you a year ago may not be even on your radar now and vice versa.

As you're working through the issues that have held you back, your values will change even faster. If you look back to what was important to you at the beginning of this book, you will see that has changed. If you're not coming from a place of fear anymore, your values will be a great deal different.

At this point, you have most of the raw ingredients to make up your foundation, but you need a few more to make it unbreakable. So, take a look back at the chart where you wrote in the number 1's and go back through it a second time. This time you'll be putting a number two next to the values you like. The difference now is that you only have to pick twenty between all that are listed and all that you wrote. It is OK to put a 2 next to some that were left blank before because even during the time you have been working on this exercise, your values will have changed. The same goes for new ones that you may want to write in. Please don't look at the values clarification chart you just did and begin to compare. There is no right or wrong in this exercise. Once you've selected all twenty, take your list of # 2's and write them in on the left, unnumbered side of the Value Prioritization chart on the next page.

> "Almost every wise saying has an opposite
> one, no less wise, to balance it."
> – George Santayana

Value Prioritization

	1. _____
_____	2. _____
_____	3. _____
_____	4. _____
_____	5. _____
_____	6. _____
_____	7. _____
_____	8. _____
_____	9. _____
_____	10. _____
_____	11. _____
_____	12. _____
_____	13. _____
_____	14. _____
_____	15. _____
_____	16. _____

_____   17. _____

_____   18. _____

_____   19. _____

_____   20. _____

Once you've done that, now rank them in order of most important to least important and write them in on the numbered side. As you transfer from the left to the right side, do yourself a favor and cross each one out as you go along. The people who don't do that inevitably write in the same one twice on the right and they can't figure out where they've gone wrong.

Now go back and compare. How many of those twenty were different than the twenty you wrote on your values clarification page? Sometimes people have had as many as sixteen different values the second time around. Once again, that's because you're doing a great deal of discerning at a very fast rate while you are really focusing on these exercises. That makes you learn and grow quite quickly.

Now, depending on what you wrote as your number one value, you may be in for a big surprise. Most people miss it entirely.

What did you pick as your #1 value on both the values clarification and the values prioritization pages? If it was anything else but *MYSELF,* you missed the point. Myself is the fourth one down on the left side of the possible values to choose from page. Did you put # 1 or # 2 by it? Did it make it to your top thirty? Did it make it to your top twenty?

You see, it's what I've been talking about through this book and a great deal in this chapter. You have to be your number one value. Without you, there are no values. You are the hub. You are the center. Everything stems from you. It doesn't matter if you wrote 'Love' in as your number one. Without you, it has no value because there is no you to value it. I can't stress this point enough. You are #1. Period. End of story.

The Power Of Integrity

This leads us into a discussion about integrity. Integrity is often misunderstood as good or bad or right or wrong. For the purposes of this discussion, I define integrity as something that is whole and complete. For example, a complete circle has integrity but if you breach the hull of a ship, you would say its hull integrity has been compromised. It just means that it is no longer perfect, whole or complete. That in itself is not good or bad, right or wrong. It just is a hole in the ship.

If you look at a bicycle tire and you removed some of its spokes, you could say the wheel is out of integrity. Well, if you look at your life and some of your values are missing, then you could say that you are out of integrity. Once again, that's not good or bad or right or wrong, it just means that your values are missing.

So, take a look at the following page and you will see a diagram of what I call your integrity circle. In each of the blank spaces, take the twenty values you just ranked and write them in the spaces. It does not matter where you begin. Just fill them all in around the circle.

As far as what goes in the center, yep you guessed it. It's MYSELF. If you were one of the rare few who selected MYSELF and put it in your values prioritization, you'll need to go back through and pick out one more value to complete your wheel.

What your integrity circle does is give you a graphic representation of what's important in your life.

MY INTEGRITY CIRCLE
The foundation of my life

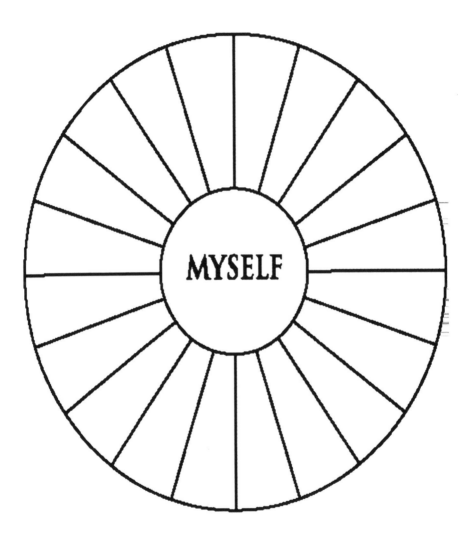

Now, you are going to do the opposite to give you something to compare this too. If you are not INtegrity, then you are OUTegrity. Now I know that's a made up word, but it serves its purpose here. On the following page is your OUTegrity circle. Take each of the words you wrote in your INtegrity circle and write in their opposites. Don't worry if it's not an exact opposite; it doesn't need to be. For example, the opposite of love for you may not be hate, it may be 'separation.' As far as what goes in the center, you'll notice there is a triangle there. I am sure you can guess why. MYSELF still goes in the center because you still are responsible for all of your values being out of place.

When you have completed these two, you should post them side by side somewhere so you can see them and use them as an autocorrect tool if your life gets out of balance. You can simply see what's missing and then take the appropriate action to help you to achieve whatever your desired outcomes are.

In addition, you should go to the website www.the24hourchampion.com and print out more of these pages because your values are going to change a great deal over the coming weeks and months as you begin to hone and refine what your life is going to look like.

MY OUTEGRITY CIRCLE
The downfalls of my life

Now I want to really congratulate you for what you've done. You know more about yourself and what's important to you than you've probably ever known. You have a foundation on which you can begin to build the rest of your life upon. From this place, you can look to your future and be able to create plans because you now have clarity and you'll be able to focus far better than you may have been able to in the past. You'll be able to achieve your goals faster and have a much better time along the way.

You should pat yourself on the back and take a break.

Know Your Top Three To Five Priorities

Getting your priorities clear is the third most essential step toward achieving a well-balanced life. The important point here is to figure out what you want your priorities to be, not what you think they should be. Since you now know what you truly value, this process will be easier.

Knowing your priorities will also help you to manage your time much more effectively. I'll be talking about that more in the next chapter. When you discover what unnecessary "priorities" you are doing that take up too much of your time and you get rid of them, you'll suddenly have much more freedom. The point is for you to drop all the stuff that no longer serves you or is not in alignment with your values.

Finally, knowing your priorities will help you to have a lot more fun and relaxation.

To help you figure out your top three to five priorities, take some time to contemplate the following question:

1. **If I gave you a box and every time you opened that box, all the money that you needed came out of it, along with all the support, all the self-esteem, all the resources and anything and everything that you needed so that you knew you couldn't fail, what would you continuously spend the money on?** After you bought all of the material things you could ever want for yourself and your family, you're only going to spend money on the things you really enjoy. Would you spend the money on travel, on charitable causes, on education? Take a few minutes now to really sit back and think about the answer to that. It is in these precious moments that you quietly look into your future and envision what you want

your life to be. Just allow the pictures to come to your mind. Spend some time imagining your life in each of those situations. Let the images fill you up with feelings of joy and fun and excitement. Allow them to sink down inside your heart and take root. Once you do that and your heart, soul and mind have expanded on that level, they can't shrink back down and allow you to settle for any less than those desires.

Whatever you came up with, write some quick notes below so you don't forget it.

_____

_____

_____

_____

_____

_____

_____

_____

Whatever you do, don't say, "I don't know." Often people drift year after year after year in their lives because they never take the time to answer that question. Usually it's because of a fear of failure or success which as we've said throughout this book is really a fear of validation of your core, negative beliefs which then threatens your survival mechanism.

If you really take the time to do this exercise properly, your top three to five will become quite apparent. You will notice patterns in the things you write down now and you will notice that you've had many of the same thoughts about your life in the past. You may see that travel comes up a lot. You may notice that a new career comes up a lot. You may see that you want to make a difference in the world in some way. You may see that you want to spend more time with your family. It really doesn't matter what you write, just as long as you take the action and begin to have those things in your life.

For illustration purposes, my top five are:

1. Being the best I can be
2. Living and sharing my love with the planet
3. Making a difference all over the world through seminars, workshops, books, audio programs, videos and so much more

4. Transforming the educational system
5. Bringing peace and love to the planet

My top 5 are in no particular order. Although, being the best I can be does have to be #1.

Knowing your top three to five priorities and taking the appropriate action to manifest them will make your life better all the way around. But I want to caution you. When you start changing your life on the level we are talking about, naturally you will be out of balance in many other areas. That's OK. It's a natural byproduct. Just take it slowly. If you try to make too many changes too quickly, you'll do yourself more harm than good and things will take longer and it will cause more stress. It's not worth it. You will get wherever you're going in due time.

> **"The truth is balance, but the opposite of truth, which is unbalance, may not be a lie."**
> **– Susan Sontag**

Establish Your Boundaries

People often don't set boundaries because they are afraid of hurting the feelings of others. Or worse yet, they are afraid that if they say, "NO" the other person will disapprove of them or not accept them or not want them or love them. So, they constantly sell themselves and their needs out. They give up what they need to do or want to do for themselves. They busy themselves with other people's wants, needs and desires running from one favor to the next. If they are insecure, they'll allow people to intrude on their personal time and to make demands of them that they don't want to do. This causes exhaustion, resentment, anger, frustration to others and to themselves. It's just a survival mechanism that doesn't need to run your life anymore. As long as you are your number one value and love, cherish, honor and respect yourself, it won't.

There are many benefits to setting proper boundaries. It often leads to greater satisfaction in work life and personal life, greater productivity, more creativity, more energy, more money, more peace of mind, more health, vitality, a better attitude, and the list goes on.

So how do you set boundaries? Go through the steps we just talked about. Once you're not worried about conflict or what other people think of you, all that's left is to simply draw the line in the sand and to make a decision not to go outside of it. For example, if you're one of those people who volunteer incessantly and it's really causing problems for you, but you haven't been able to say, "NO", here is what you do. Cut the hours down to half or a third or a quarter of what you were doing. And then don't allow yourself to get off that track. Make the decision and then commit to it. And it is the same for every other area in your life, your business or both. Make the decisions you don't want to make and then don't back out of them. It may be hard at first. People in your life may not like it, but your life and your time and what you do with it is your business.

A Closing Thought

The art of balance is truly that. It's an art. Things will be out of balance many times in your life. Yet, there is a balance to balance. You must look at the big picture to really see if your life is balanced or not. Don't judge or beat yourself up if things are out of balance temporarily. Striving for perfect balance will cause insanity. There's no way to have it. Life is a balancing act. Sometimes the pendulum will have to swing in the opposite direction for a while. And that's O.K. As long as you know what's really important to you (your personal values) and what your top priorities are in life and you've learned the very important lesson of being able to say NO, your life will be much more in balance and things will flow smoother, you'll be happier, you'll have more energy, more time, better health, improved relationships and you'll have a lot more fun along the way.

Summary Of Key Ideas And Important Points

1. Perfect balance is an illusion just as perfectionism is. They are both impossible.
2. There is a balance within balance.
3. Things may be out of balance while you're putting your life in balance. That's OK.

4. The better you know yourself, the more easily you'll be able to balance your life.

5. Keep reexamining your values. They will change frequently as your life changes.

6. Make balancing your life a game. In other words, don't take it so seriously.

7. Focus on yourself, your wants and your needs. Take care of them first.

8. When one section of your life is out of balance, it often throws the others off. Take care of that one first and the rest will fall into place much easier.

9. It's not just OK, it's imperative that you set proper boundaries and say, "NO!"

10. Schedule your priorities. Don't prioritize your schedule.

CHAPTER 9

ACTION! ACTION! ACTION!

"Dreams pass into the reality of action. From the actions stems the dream again; and this interdependence produces the highest form of living." – Anais Nin

So far, the focus of this book has been about the inner work of being a champion. It has focused on the first step in the creation process (the being part). This chapter's focus will mainly be about step two (the doing part). Step three (having) will be the result in your life after you do the first two.

This is where the entire book comes together and literally what will make or break your success. Without the proper action, all the rest of this book is meaningless. Yet so many people will stop at this point. I have met hundreds and hundreds of people over the years who go to seminar after seminar, workshop after workshop, year after year and never change. They keep working on themselves so they can avoid living their life. They're willing to do all the 'hard' work of personal growth without the reward of experiencing a new life. You look at their lives (behind the scenes) and they're a mess, but they look good to all outward appearances. They make a great deal of noise about wanting to change, but they really don't. So they never take the appropriate action.

Now, you are at that point as well. You have a choice. You can stay where you are or move ahead. You can be the champion you were born to be or you can be something less. You can be a victor or you can be a victim. Your time is now. The fact of the matter is that you've taken huge leaps to creating a brand new life. You've done more work on yourself than most people ever will. You've stepped out of your comfort zone and are about to step into a brand new reality. In order to make sure that all the work you've done has not been in vain, you have to take appropriate, laser focused, massive action. After all, that is why you're reading this, isn't it? You want your dream life now, don't you?

One of the action steps you must take is to learn to think like wealthy people think. I put this first because when you start to train yourself to think this way, your personality begins to change. What was impossible now becomes possible. The world begins to open up. The things you want don't seem out of reach. Life becomes a little easier.

To help you to start that process, here are some ideas to consider. Now, you may or may not agree with all of them and that's OK. This list is by no means exhaustive. However, if you take just one or two nuggets of information, you can then parlay that into a fortune. The following list comes from my experiences of working with people who have earned their money by being entrepreneurs and good business people.

> ## "Whatever you can do, or dream you can, begin it. Boldness has genius, power and magic in it."
> ## – Johann Wolfgang Von Goethe

Some Ideas about 'Conscious' Wealthy People And How They Think About Money

$ Money is just a tool to them and they know how to use the tool.

$ They often do what they love knowing that the money will follow. And when they do what they love, what they do is not like work, it's more like fun.

$ They don't make excuses for their failures. They don't let fear block them, stop them or deter them.

$ They believe in themselves. They believe in what they do and take immediate, appropriate, massive, laser focused action to accomplish their goals and plans. They go the extra mile. They know that if they do more than they are paid for, they will soon be paid for more than they do.

$ They are responsible for their finances.

$ They are always on the lookout for opportunities and grab them quickly when one comes their way.

$ They are always promoting themselves because they believe in themselves and what they do and they know that if they don't share that with the world, it will be doing the world a disservice.

$ They know that regardless of the business they are in, their main business is selling and marketing. Nothing happens until something is sold, so they are always selling.

$ Wealthy people get paid by what they produce, not for how long they spend producing it or how hard or how long they work. They don't believe in trading hours for dollars.

$ Wealthy people are responsible to themselves and for their dreams. They are committed to their success. They do what they say they are going to do and they don't back out. They don't give up. They don't quit. They don't sell themselves or their dreams short.

$ They are creative and passionate. They have a zest for life and living. They take risks, knowing that with big risks, come big rewards. In short, they are always focusing on how to get where they're going.

$ They are win-win focused. They know that when everyone wins, everyone makes more, so they are team players.

$ They are not concerned with holding tightly to what they have because they know that stops the flow of abundance coming to them.

$ They are intelligent. They are open-minded and as a result, they easily change their habits.

$ They know they can have whatever they want as long as they are willing to work for it. They know they deserve wealth. They don't take no for an answer.

$ They have a winning attitude. They have magnetic personalities and they easily attract the people and circumstances that move their business and their lives in the direction they want them to go.

$ Wealthy people visualize their success and know that everything they are intending is already theirs because they are in harmony with the Universe. They expect success. They are clear about what they want and they don't send out mixed signals to the Universe. They first see what they want in their mind's eye. Then they allow the Universe to do its job and provide what they ask for. That is, they use the law of attraction to their greatest advantage.

$ They don't live in the past and dwell on their mistakes or sit on the fence. They know that their past has passed and that their future is a blank tablet on which they can write in whatever they believe they can have. This is why they keep getting richer. They are decisive and make decisions quickly while they are moving ahead. If they fail, they do it while they are moving ahead and they do it quickly.

All of those character traits of conscious, wealthy people are all well and good, but as I have said several times in this book, they will make no difference unless you take the time to really study them and make them a part of your psyche. What you can do is write them down and read them at least once a day, preferably more. Then, as you keep growing and learning, add to them. Rewrite them. Make them your own. In other words, write them down in the first person (I language) and in the present tense.

The next powerful action step to take is to learn how to set, write and achieve any goal.

> ## "Don't measure busywork. Don't measure activity. Measure accomplishment. It doesn't matter what people do as much as it matters what they get done."
> ### – Larry Winget

Goal Setting For Ultimate Success

For years I resisted setting goals. I didn't believe in them. I thought they were a waste of time. I didn't think they were very valuable. In reality, I thought they were useless. The reason was simple. I didn't believe in myself, nor did I think myself worthy enough to deserve to have what I wanted. I would set all kinds of goals for myself knowing full well that I wasn't going to ever reach them. I was dead in the water. I never had a prayer. It was over before it began.

Of course, that has all changed now and that is the intention for you as well. So for those of you who have worked on goals previously, before you roll your eyes and say, "Uuuuugggggggghhhhhhh!!!!! And before you make up your mind that you're not going to do them, stop yourself right there and immediately start thinking like a champion. Now that your unconscious beliefs are not sabotaging your every move, now that you believe in yourself, now that you are taking full responsibility for everything you're thinking and feeling, now that you're committed, now that you're trusting your gut the whole way and coming from a place of love, goal setting and more importantly, goal achieving will be much easier.

For those of you who are new to setting goals, think of it like this: If a professional sports team has no goal of being world champions, what's the point? If each coach doesn't have a goal of bringing out the winner in all of his players, he's got no business coaching. If each player doesn't strive to be the best he can be, he shouldn't be playing.

If you don't have the end in mind, you won't ever get there. And if you don't know where you're going, any road will take you there. What goals do is give you something to reach for, something to pull you along, something to believe in.

I came up with an acronym for G.O.A.L.S. It is:

Guaranteed
Outcomes
Achieved by
Little
Steps

If you look at goals from that perspective, they are quite easy. The outcomes are guaranteed if you just take little steps, slowly nibbling away at the project until it's complete.

After nearly two decades of working with people, I have realized that the majority of them had only a vague concept of what a goal is. So I put together this list to make the whole process of goal achieving much easier.

Goal Achieving Checklist

☑ *__Your goals must be for you.__* In other words, you must do them for you. The reason is that they must be real and relevant to you or they won't be right for you.

☑ *__You must know why you have those goals__*. It's doubtful that you will hear anyone who teaches goal setting tell you about this step. Yet, this is the most critical step of all because knowing why will motivate you into action on a daily basis. It will get you past any blocks or fears and keep your thoughts and feelings focused in a positive direction, totally on course. Knowing why is literally the foundation of your goals and plans. A goal without a why is not any better than a pipe dream.

☑ *__Your goals must be fun__*. Create goals that uplift, inspire, bring joy, fulfillment and satisfaction to you, not hard work.

☑ *__Your goals should be clear__*. They should be simple, clearly defined and straightforward.

☑ *__Your goals must be well-balanced__*. As you saw in the last chapter, when things get out of balance, life gets very difficult.

☑ *__Your goals must inspire you__*. You must truly love them. The more they mean, the more motivation, inspiration and creativity you will have.

☑ *__Your goals must be flexible__*. Flexibility keeps you from feeling overwhelmed, overworked, overburdened. Like a Weeping Willow tree in a violent storm, flexible goals allow you to go with the flow and not snap and break under the pressure.

☑ ***You must believe you can achieve them***. As you think, so shall you be. It is the same for your goals. If you don't believe in yourself or your goals, you will never achieve them.

☑ ***You must assume full responsibility for their completion.*** It is not ever someone else's fault or something else's fault if you don't accomplish your goals. It is not even your own fault. It is however, always your responsibility.

☑ ***You must be 100% committed to reaching them***. 99.9% commitment is equal to 0%. Don't fool yourself into thinking it's any more than that. You must be prepared to give up some things to make your goals become a reality. When you commit, which is by definition 100%, you will have many benefits and unexpected resources show up to help you in your commitment.

☑ ***Your goals must be specific and measurable and written***. Depending on the goal, the more concrete, the better. This enables you to chunk your action steps down into easily manageable parts. In addition, writing them down makes them more real. It gives them life and also much easier to keep track of.

☑ ***Your goals must be challenging***. They must stretch you, but they must be doable. The point is, you're not going to be an NFL linebacker if you're 5'6" and weigh 180. But, you could be a receiver. Also, wimpy goals do nothing for anyone. For all intents and purposes, they are meaningless.

☑ ***Your goals must be in alignment and congruent with your values***. It simply doesn't make sense to set goals that are in direct opposition to what's really important to you. If you do go against your values, it will be like trying to push a rope uphill, extremely difficult if not impossible.

☑ ***Your goals must be in alignment with your intuition***. Pay attention to your gut no matter what. If your gut says no, then don't go.

☑ ***Your goals must be a team effort***. Tell only those people who will give you nothing but positive encouragement. Often times this is not your family.

Although they may be well meaning, they often will bring you down while trying to help you by telling you what they think is best for you.

☑ *You must be able to take appropriate, laser focused, massive action in order to achieve them.* Without action, everything falls apart.

Now that you have a basic understanding of what goals are, how to use them and how to work them, it's time to set some of your own. I would suggest that you start small. Build up slowly. If you're beginning a new exercise program, set your first goal of joining a gym. If you're already a member, just set a goal of going one time. Do yourself a favor and don't knock that idea thinking it won't work to go only once. When you're beginning anything new, sometimes the hardest part is getting started. If your ultimate goal is to lose one hundred pounds, then your intermediate goals might look something like this:

OVERALL GOAL (The Big Picture) – LOSE 100 POUNDS IN ONE YEAR

1st Intermediate Goal - Lose thirty-six pounds (an average of three pounds a week) in the healthiest manner possible for the first twelve weeks while not starving to death, depriving myself of rewards once in a while, working to death or beating my body down.

1. Join a gym now
2. Hire a personal trainer
3. Read several books on different types of exercise
4. Read several books on nutrition
5. Lose three pounds week # one
6. Lose five pounds week # two
7. Lose six pounds week # three
8. Take a break week # four and just maintain
9. Lose four pounds week # five
10. Change my workout routine to confuse my muscles in week # six
11. Lose three pounds week seven
12. Lose another three pounds in week eight
13. Lose another three pounds a week for the next four weeks

2nd Intermediate Goal – Lose forty-two pounds over the next quarter in the healthiest manner possible while not starving to death, depriving myself of rewards once in a while, working to death or beating my body down.

I have not written all the individual steps like the thirteen above as it is not important to convey the idea. In reality you would come up with your own number of steps and what you would do in each one.

3rd Intermediate Goal – Lose twenty-two pounds over the final quarter in the healthiest manner possible while not starving to death, depriving myself of rewards once in a while, working to death or beating my body down.

How does that feel? Those goals are specific, measurable, doable, clear, etc., etc. Anyone that's healthy enough and has a real desire could do that. That's the point. When you set them, you say to yourself, "I can do that."

Disclaimer. I am not a licensed or trained nutritionist or exercise instructor. My example was for illustrative purposes only and should not be taken as sound, medical advice. Before starting any diet or exercise program, be sure to consult your doctor.

What's Your Goal?

Now it's your turn. Pick something you want to do that you have been putting off for whatever reason. Maybe you want to learn an instrument. Maybe you want to start a new career. Maybe you have a project at work that has been handed to you and you need to break it down. Maybe you're single and your goal is to be dating three times a week or maybe it's to find your perfect mate. Whatever it is, here's your chance to get it down on paper. When you do that, it will build up your energy, your drive, your motivation and you'll be inspired to take action which we will talk about in the next section.

My overall (big picture) goal

My first intermediate goal

1._____
2._____
3._____
4._____
5._____

My second intermediate goal

_____
_____
_____

1._____
2._____
3._____
4._____
5._____

My third intermediate goal

_____
_____
_____

1._____
2._____
3._____
4._____
5._____

Congratulations! You've done it. Pat yourself on the back. Let's keep the momentum going by writing an action plan to ensure that the goals you just wrote turn into reality.

The following section will help you to understand what an action plan is and what it should consist of, why you need to write one and how to do it in the quickest manner possible.

Why People Avoid Writing An Action Plan And How To Overcome That Avoidance And Write One Quickly And Easily

When it comes to writing down a plan, it can sometimes seem very difficult. There are so many variables to consider and so many unknowns to contend with. In addition, sometimes it appears hard to take a big idea and break it down into manageable parts. Some people don't want to be held accountable to what they've written. Some people don't want to write an action plan because they have a fear that they may actually succeed. Some have a fear that they may fail. Some don't feel good enough or that they deserve success. Some people don't want to feel like they are trapped to what they've written.

I know that was the way I felt. I didn't want to be told what to do even if it was me doing the telling. If any of those applied to you, congratulations, they are done and over. I also believe that people don't write action plans, because like goals, they haven't been taught how easy they actually are. They end up getting confused about what action plans are, how to start them, what's in them and why they should even do one in the first place. So let's make it simple. This will clear up all of those questions and make writing an action plan much quicker and easier.

What is an Action Plan?

An action plan is just written steps to accomplish a given task within a given period of time and it answers the who's, what's, when's, where's, why's and how's. Don't make it any harder. They must be clear, straightforward and easy to follow. They must be doable. They must have deadlines and accountability measures.

The following explanation will break down the action plan so it's clear and easy to understand.

An Action Plan Explanation

- **Step One – The Objective** - What do you want to achieve from writing this plan? In other words, what's the overall goal? If you did the goal setting exercise earlier, just write your overall, big picture goal and write it clearly and succinctly.

- **Step Two –The Reason(s)** - These are all of the reasons why you want your goal. The important step here is to clearly write down the WHY. Don't just think about it. If the why is big enough, the how, will take care of itself. This is one of the most important steps. Knowing why is what will motivate you, energize you, inspire you and make you want to get beyond any blocks, fears, doubts or setbacks. Spend as much time on this step as you need.

- **Step Three – The Strategies** - This is where you list between three to five general strategies or approaches you will take to achieve your objective.

- **Step Four – The Tactics and Times** - Break down the strategies into specific tactics (steps). List when all tasks involved will be done. Be very specific and include deadlines.

- **Step Five – The Accountability Points and Landmarks** – This is all about measuring and rewarding progress and helps keep you accountable along the way. You can establish daily, weekly or monthly accountability points to help you reach your landmarks.

It really is that simple. A good action plan should take less than an hour to write and probably closer to thirty-minutes. For illustration purposes, I have included an actual simplified version of an action plan that I have written and one that I am currently (as of March of 2009) using to promote this book.

> ## "Obstacles are what unsuccessful people see on their way to failure."
> ### – Darshan Shanti

Darshan's Action Plan

1. **OBJECTIVE** – Having <u>The 24-Hour Champion</u> become a # 1 N.Y. Times Best Seller and #1 on Amazon.com.

2. **WHY** – This is the continuation of a lifelong dream to have a world renowned personal development company that through its seminars, workshops, books, CD programs, music, poetry etc., reaches millions and millions of people all over the globe. For me, this is pure joy. This is my purpose. This is the only thing that truly satisfies me. I would not enjoy my life if I could not do this. In fact, it wouldn't be worth living if I could not pursue this passion.

3. **STRATEGIES**
    1. Learn the business of publishing
    2. Increase marketing on the internet
    3. Establish a big PR campaign.

4. **TACTICS AND TIMES**
    1. Learn the business of publishing - March-December 2009
    - Attend book marketing seminars when they are given
    - Buy books and reports and learn from successful authors - 2009
    - Network with other authors – March-December 2009
    - Research literary agents and hire one if applicable – 2009
    - Research and apply for grants if applicable – March -December 2009

2. **Increase my marketing on the internet** - Ongoing
    - Start a Google Ad Words Campaign – March 2009
    - Create an e-book version – January 2009
    - Start and run an affiliate marketing campaign - March 2009
    - Get listed on dozens of other people's sites – March-December 2009
    - Create a Facebook page that markets my book - 2009
    - Build a Search Engine Optimized website to market and sell the book – April 2009
    - Write a sales letter for the book and post it on the web – January 2009

3. **Establish a huge PR campaign** – January 2009
   - Go on local radio - January-December 2009
   - Go on internet radio - January-December 2009
   - Go on local TV - January-December 2009
   - Have an article or two written about the book in various local papers – May 2009
   - Write articles for local and national papers and magazines - January-December 2009
   - Do many local talks and book signings – January - December 2009... and beyond

5. **ACCOUNTABILITY POINTS AND LANDMARKS**
   1. By March of 2009, have at least one article published about the book
   2. Submit articles to five different magazines, newspapers, etc. that would have a readership looking for what I offer.
      A. By May or June of 2009, have at least two book signings at local bookstores
      1. Call or visit five local bookstores and talk with the staff

      B. By June of 2009, have sold at least 500 copies
      1. Sell 100 in April
      2. Sell 200 in May
      3. Sel 200 in June

      C. By November of 2009, have done at least ten book signings
      1. Do one in August
      2. Do two in September
      3. Do four in October
      4. Do three in November

      D. By December of 2009, have sold at least 20,000 copies all over the country and on Amazon.com
      1. Sell 1,000 in August
      2. Sell 2,000 in September
      3. Sell 5,000 in October
      4. Sell 5,000 in November
      5. Sell 7,000 in December

When a plan is broken down like this and each step can be seen clearly, it enables you to avoid being overwhelmed. It enables you to accomplish each step and gain confidence and inner strength along the way.

Just take this example and create your own. Don't give up. You will be surprised how easy it really is and how quickly you can do it and how many new ideas come to you.

Your Action Plan Template

YOUR OBJECTIVE –

_____

_____

_____

WHY YOU WANT TO DO IT –

_____

_____

_____

YOUR STRATEGIES

1._____
2._____
3._____
4._____
5._____

YOUR TACTICS AND TIMES FOR THEIR COMPLETION

1._____

-
-
-
-
-

2. _____

-
-
-
-
-

3. _____

-
-
-
-
-

4. _____

-
-
-
-
-

5. _____

-
-
-
-
-

YOUR ACCOUNTABILITY POINTS AND THEIR LANDMARKS

LANDMARK 1 - _____

Accountability Points to meet Landmark 1

1._____
2._____
3._____

Landmark 2 - _____

Accountability Points to meet Landmark 2
1._____
2._____
3._____

Landmark 3 - _____

Accountability Points to meet Landmark 3
1._____
2._____
3._____

There it is. If you have accomplished this task, then you've done a lot of the work already. You've done the hard part. You've organized your thoughts and put them into motion. Now that the ball is rolling, it will get easier and easier to keep it rolling. The momentum is now on your side. This next section is going to help you to make time work for you not against you.

Time Management Demystified

> "It's not so much how busy you are, but why you are busy. The bee is praised. The mosquito is swatted."
> – Mary O'Connor

I know many people who are very, very busy. I was one of them for many years. They barely have time to breathe let alone anything else. They run around doing, doing and doing and get virtually nothing accomplished. They may be busy, but they are not productive. It costs them time, money, stress and confusion. They are confounded with the fact that they are always buried in work and no matter what they do, they can't ever dig themselves out. Does that sound like you or someone you know? Well there is no reason for it as you're about to find out.

There is no such thing as time management. I have said for years and years that people don't have a time management problem, they have a priority management problem. The point is, you have to schedule your priorities. It's not the amount of time you have that's the issue, it's what you deem to be most important and spend your time doing that is the issue. So, if you're one of those people who can't ever seem to find the time to get the things done that you really want to, look at what you're making most important. Many times people never get to the things they really want to do because they make everyone and everything else a priority.

Ultimately it always comes down to your decisions. I always ask people, "If I paid you $1,000.00 a day to do that tiny ten minute task that you can never get to, would you have a problem getting to it?" Of course, they say no. Right then and there they have their answer. They had the time, they just didn't make what they said they wanted to do a big enough priority. Now, I do understand that sometimes there are time constraints and it is not always possible to get everything done that needs to be done. However, that is the exception, not the rule.

The Priority Management System

If you're having trouble managing your priorities or scheduling your time, one of the most effective systems I have ever found for getting more done, easier and faster is this. Just write down the six most important things you have to do that day and do each one of them until it is complete. In other words, don't move on to number two unless number one is finished. Now if you get to the point on number one where you are waiting for someone in order to be able to finish it, then you can move on to number two. Then go back to number one immediately when what you were waiting for has arrived. Finish it and then go back to number two. Finish that and then work your way down the list. You will be amazed at how much more productive you are.

The Priority Question

Here is one single question that will act as your productivity meter. If you're honest as you ask yourself the question, you'll immediately know if you're on or off track. It will also help you to know if the six things you've written down are going to be the best use of your time. Remember, it's easy to do the little things because it looks like you're getting a lot accomplished, but in the grand scheme of things, you're really getting much less accomplished than you could. Tackle the bigger, more important tasks first and then the little stuff. Just ask yourself this question.

IS WHAT I'M DOING RIGHT NOW BRINGING ME CLOSER TO OR TAKING ME FURTHER AWAY FROM MY GOALS OR THE THINGS I WANT?

If it's further away, stop it immediately and do what you need to do. It may not be the most fun. It may be more challenging. It may be difficult. Do it anyway. Champions are productive. They work very smart while working hard and they get much more done that way. You are a champion.

Persevere While You Create Your Future

Finally, what sets champions apart from everyone else is that they never give up. So many people get all the way to the 99 yard line and stop right there. They never experience the joy of the touchdown.

But champions don't quit. They keep going in spite of tremendous odds. They persevere. They keep moving forward even when the results they want are not happening at nearly the speed they would like. They know that although it may be very hard at times to continue because of rejection, no or slow progress, frustration, aggravation, confusion, they must not quit.

Perseverance is a trait shared by the most successful people in the world. When the going got tough, they got tougher. They began to do more and more. They buckled down. They tightened up all the loose ends, cleared away all the unnecessary time wasters and distractions, rolled up their sleeves and they went to work.

These successful people are able to persevere because of where their focus is. They keep their eyes on where they are going, not where they've been. They see the big picture. They have no problem losing a few battles because they know they will win the war.

One of the best examples of perseverance is this question.

Would you rather have a million dollars right now or a penny that was doubled and then doubled and then doubled, etc. everyday for a month? If you would rather have the million dollars, you'd lose a great deal. If that sounds crazy, just do the math.

Day 1 = .01
Day 2 = .02
Day 3 = .04
Day 4 = .08
Day 5 = .16
Day 6 = .32
Day 7 = .64
Day 8 = 1.28
Day 9 = 2.56
Day 10 = 5.12
Day 11 = 10.24
Day 12 = 20.48
Day 13 = 40.96
Day 14 = 81.92
Day 15 = 163.84
Day 16 = 327.68
Day 17 = 655.36
Day 18 = 1,310.72
Day 19 = 2,621.44
Day 20 = 5,242.88
Day 21 = 10,485.76
Day 22 = 20,971.52
Day 23 = 41,943.04
Day 24 = 83,886.08
Day 25 = 167,772.16
Day 26 = 335,544.32
Day 27 = 671,088.64
Day 28 = 1,342,177.28
Day 29 = 2,684,354.56
Day 30 = 5,368,709.12
Day 31 = 10,737,418.24

The point is, perseverance pays off big time. Most people would have quit by day ten or fifteen. A few would have stuck it out to day twenty. But the champions whose eyes were on the prize, who never lost site and hung in there, became richer than their wildest dreams. They didn't take the easy way out no matter how tempting it was. As a result they were truly victorious.

> ## "If you don't design your own life plan, chances are you'll fall into someone else's plan. And guess what they have planned for you? Not much."
> ### – Jim Rohn

Summary Of Key Ideas And Important Points

1. Wealthy people think differently than those without money. Think like them and take the appropriate, continuous action and you'll be able to live like them.
2. Richness is a state of mind.
3. Being broke is temporary. Being poor minded is a disease you don't want to catch.
4. People with no commitment to their success, set no goals.
5. Goals are virtually useless if done incorrectly.
6. Goals should be like a magnet that's always pulling you forward.
7. An idea will only ever be an idea without the energy of action behind it.
8. Take action immediately and consistently on your goals.
9. The right action is critical. - Being busy is very different than being productive.
10. Don't ever give up. Ever. Ever. Ever.

AFTERWORD

YOU are about to enter into a fascinating journey of self-discovery. That journey will take YOU places and enable YOU to experience things that YOU previously thought unimaginable. YOU are now going to live as a champion, a 24-hour champion. YOU can sit back and be an observer or YOU can actively steer YOUR ship where YOU want it to go. The decision is completely up to YOU. There is nothing in YOUR way anymore. The land mines and obstacles (YOUR self-limiting, unconscious beliefs), blocking YOU have been cleared. And YOU now have the tools to clear away any future blocks and blast them to smithereens. YOU have an unlimited supply of fuel (YOUR creativity and imagination and power) and a ship that is designed to last for many more decades. It is impenetrable from outside attack, but 100% vulnerable from self-sabotage (Fear, giving it the wrong food, not exercising its motors enough).

YOUR life awaits. YOUR dreams await. YOUR happiness and joy and satisfaction have been put off for far too long. The time for YOU is now. YOU have turned the corner and are now gaining speed. YOU no longer hold back. Where will YOU go? What will YOU do? How much will YOU see? YOU now have many choices that did not exist before. What will YOU decide? YOUR future is completely in YOUR hands.

It has been my great honor and privilege to write this book. I hope it has served you well and will continue to do so in the future.

ABOUT THE AUTHOR

Hello my friend,

My name is Darshan Gabriel Shanti. That is my chosen, spiritual name. Darshan is a Hindi word that roughly translates into, 'Being in the presence of a holy person,' 'One who sees God in all people,' 'Vision.' My middle name was given to me by my princess Ajanel. Shanti is also a Hindi word. It means peace. My name calls me into being. Like I always say, "If I don't see good things in all people, I'm in the wrong business." My name is the essence of who I am and what I do. My mission is to bring peace to this planet through individual self-awareness by helping people to realize their magnificence, their greatness and their pricelessness and that the truth of them is love... nothing less. I have dedicated the rest of my life to that mission. I will fulfill that mission through my upcoming books, video and audio programs, my poetry, my live seminars and workshops and The World's Love Project.

I am blessed to have been able to write this book and share this information with you. One day, perhaps our paths will cross and you can share the miracle of your life with me. Until such time, I wish you well on your journey.

Love,
Darshan G. Shanti
July 7, 2008 6:55 PM MST

RESOURCES

These are priceless resources that I have discovered (and used) over the years to help me make my business a success. Without them, it would have taken me years longer, tons of stress, a great deal of aggravation and pain and a heck of a lot more money.

Learn from my mistakes and don't make the same ones. I've done the work already and found these great resources. Use them and you won't be disappointed.

www.clientattraction.com - If you're struggling to attract clients or business and no matter what you've done, it's not working, this is the program for you.

www.marketingdemystified.com - If you've pulled your hair out trying to understand marketing and you want to cut right through all the B.S. that's all over the internet, then go at once to this site.

www.aweber.com - If you are looking to start writing newsletters on the internet or you want to do email marketing, this is the best company I've found.

www.1and1.com - If you want to build your own website and you're a complete novice or an expert, this is a fantastic company to work with for the cheapest prices I've found.

www.musivation.com – One of the greatest ways you can reprogram your mind for winning is through music. Go through this site and get all that you can. There are literally dozens and dozens of resources on every subject related to your personal development. Soon you'll be singing your way to success.

www.wholesaleprinted.com – This printing service produced the best business cards I've ever had and is one of the most cost effective I have ever found. Any kind of printing from business cards to catalogs to posters, they can do. Their turnaround is very fast and their quality is excellent.

An Opportunity To Be Supported By Darshan's Other Books

The Possible You – 52 Inspiring Poems
On Life And Living Your Dreams

This is not a book of traditional poetry. On the contrary, it is a book of deeply meaningful, personal growth messages that just happen to rhyme. I spent years of my life writing these and I decided to put them together in a collection. They are all original and they are all from my deep, personal challenges in being a conscious human being. The poems will make you think, make you cry, make you laugh and make you sigh. They will warm your heart and your soul. Helping you grow is this book's goal. $29.95

The 10 BIGGEST Lies – How We've Programmed Ourselves To Fail Without Knowing It and What We Can Do To Instantly And Permanently Turn That Around

How many times do we lie to ourselves about what we can and can't do? How many times do we settle for less than we really want? How many times do we justify our goals and dreams and happiness away? When you discover and then stop telling yourself the lies that are so prevalent in society, yet so hidden to yourself, you can begin to reverse it immediately and you won't be programming yourself to fail anymore. $12.95

To place an order, visit www.foreverfreetobe.com or call (505) – 321-4914 or send an email to darshan@foreverfreetobe.com
Quantity Discounts Are Available